*The Clown, from Heart to Heart*

The Clown, from Heart to Heart
© 2011 Ton Kurstjens, Nijmegen, The Netherlands

Publication: Ton Kurstjens Clownerie
  *ton@clownerie.nl*
  *www.clownerie.nl*

Cover photography: Margit Oellers, Düsseldorf *(front)*
  Onno van Geuns *(back)*

Translation: Cécile Nowack and Thamar Elissen — *Dutch editors*
  Amy Hoogstraten, Anneke Comello, Brenda Jacobs and
  Carien Knol, Radboud University Nijmegen
  for the translation, under the supervision of
  Drs. P.J.E. Hyams — *initial translators*
  Isa McKechnie — *final translator & native speaker, www.sryver.nl*

Design/layout: FormMatters: Bart Roelofs
  *info@formmatters.nl*
  *www.formmatters.nl*

ISBN: 978-1-907611-62-9

# The Clown, from Heart to Heart

Ton Kurstjens

# Content

# Preface and Acknowledgements

*t*he title of this book is *The clown, from Heart to Heart*. The title relates to my personal clown, who wants to move people with his heart. This book is a combination of the earlier published Dutch books *De clown, een wandelend hart* (not translated) and *De clown, het innerlijke kind* (not translated). In this publication, parts have been left out or rewritten and new material has been added.

Everywhere you read 'he', you can also read 'she'.

In order to shape this book to what I had in mind, I asked for and received valuable contributions from several people, for which I am most grateful.

I would like to thank Bart Roelofs for the layout, Cécile Nowack and Thamar Elissen for editing in Dutch, and Amy Hoogstraten, Anneke Comello, Brenda Jacobs and Carien Knol, Radboud University of Nijmegen for the initial translation, under the supervision of Drs. P.J.E. Hyams.

Next, I thank Sabine Schönauer for corrections and Isa McKechnie for the final translation, superb suggestions and patience.

More thanks go out to Manuel van Baarsen, Eva van Ginkel, Jan Hiel, Meino van Kesteren, Annemieke van Melzen, Mariët Mensink, Anne Stijn van Nes, and Mandy van der Zeeuw for reading and suggestions.

Thanks to the people who shared their wonderful impressions that are included at the end of this book.

I also thank my children, Roos and Steef, for reading and (computer) support.

Last but not least I thank my brave course participants for their faith, inspiration and authenticity.

I dedicate this book to all clowns who truly dare to show their vulnerability, and to everyone pursuing their desires.

*Ton Kurstjens, January 2011*

# Introduction

Clowning is fun! A clown fantasises, discovers, tries, surprises, dares, experiences. Everything bubbles and fizzles and sometimes your stomach hurts from laughing so much. Being a clown is an invitation for you to empower yourself, empty your busy head, and get to the source of the energy in your belly.

A clown is transparent. He knows no double meanings, sarcasm or cynicism. He helps you see and experience that spontaneity is a basic strength and that you do not need to be perfect.
He is naive and open like a child, and from this starting point he connects with his environment. A clown shows you how enjoyable it can be to have unconstrained fun, act on your impulses, and show your feelings freely.

Why does a clown behave the way he does, and why do some people enjoy clowning so much? What is the source of the satisfaction? To me, clowning is about intensely experiencing freedom, about childlike playfulness, and about conquering fears. As a clown I have experienced how wonderful it is to let my imagination run wild without thinking (too much) about the consequences. I am allowed to exaggerate, to be impulsive, unrestrained, and grotesque. Everything is possible. Better yet: peolple even encourage it. Clowning makes the energy in my body flow and sparkle.

To some people the thought of such an experience may seem miles away. I often provide the participants of my clowning courses with the image of a big and shiny Olympic medal, dangling on their chests. As a result, their chests are automatically raised and their shoulders go back, which creates an open posture. This comes with a feeling of pride, and perhaps even more so, a feeling of happiness. Clowns radiate pure joy of living. In the words of my clown colleague Meino, 'the clown is light and happy like a child with a new pair of shoes!'

There are many obstacles which prevent people from living freely. As adults we appear to be more capable of bearing judgments than we were during our sensitive younger years. The soul is calloused and we have shields drawn up to protect us. The desire for more freedom and playfulness is overshadowed by expectations (from others and from ourselves), judgments and social duties.
What can we do to make ourselves happier? Friends could help us, but do we dare to open our hearts to them? A therapist could help us, but do we dare to take that step? Books give insights, but how do we apply this knowledge to our own lives? Because of fear, we tend to discard responsibility for our own happiness, and we maintain our barriers. There is too much fear of change, fear of old pain resurfacing, and fear of being too vulnerable.

Little children provide us with examples of what it can be like to live life from love. There are no opinions or judgements yet; there is merely spontaneity and joy of living. Children are often fascinating to watch. Research shows that toddlers laugh approximately 400 times a day, adults only 15 times. That's no laughing matter! Don't we all want to enjoy life the way children do? We have a great natural longing for fun, but we often do not act on our desires. Personally, I know I am sometimes not able to enjoy 'happy' moments. Either I simply look ahead, or a little puritan voice in my head keeps telling me that I do not deserve this.

I have experienced that many people, including myself, find that making genuine contact can be difficult. People communicate differently and this sometimes results in firm beliefs and set patterns of life. As we grow older, we gain a better understanding of our restrictions. Sooner or later we will long for that bygone freedom. We develop more insight into what we are like and what we want to do in life in order to continue developing. When we reach this point, it becomes a challenge – or maybe even a task – to learn how to freely express our blocked emotions. To dare to act on our desires and let our hearts speak; without expectations, prejudices, or reservations. In my opinion, we need to face our fears before we can leave them behind. We need to reflect on ourselves and on our ego, our ambitions to succeed, and our tenacity. 'Letting go' is the key to making contact, first with ourselves, and subsequently with the people who surround us. Only then are we ready to really connect.

Being a childlike clown can help us restore the connection with our inner child. This way, we can experience the same freedom and fun we once knew when we were playful children. During my clowning courses, I sometimes see people break loose from their restraints and thoroughly enjoy the freedom that surfaces. Such energy, such fun! Playing from a sense of joy, that is what this book is all about.

In this book I may portray a clown in only one particular way. I do this because this particular clown and his way of performing best fit my own ideas. However, this does not mean that I deny the many other kinds of clowns or types of clowning. I make a distinction between an 'improvising' clown and a 'theatrical' clown, although of course there are also combinations of both types. An improvising clown lets his performance spring from the present moment and he shows his emotions openly to the people around him. Performances of a theatrical clown are grander and his acts are often prepared beforehand. In this book I will mostly discuss improvising clowns.

When supervising a clown, I try to encourage actions that come from within, and tend to give little focus to the outside (clothes, makeup, attributes). I often ask, 'what does the clown feel?' instead of, 'what does he look like?' I am looking for a clown's unique and vulnerable personality. I am looking for a clown who acts spontaneously, based on what his heart tells him to do, with the intention to have a good time with the people that surround him. Clowns performing in this way are often called 'gentle clowns'. They are friendly, they care about their environment, and they make heartfelt contact. They need little: a happy mood, a friendly glance, a brief touch. When a clowns plays from the heart, he will open a heart.

Chapter 1, THE CLOWN, gives background information on the clown's persona and describes the clown as a character.

Chapter 2, WHAT TYPE OF CLOWN ARE YOU?, offers insights and exercises to explore your own clown.

Chapter 3, RETURNING TO THE INNER CHILD, explores the experiences of children and leads you back to your own childlike imagination and perceptions.

Chapter 4, FEELING AND INTUITION, gives attention to emotions and intuition, which are important instruments to use when clowning.

Chapter 5, PLAYING WITH THE AUDIENCE, contains practical tips and exercises how to perform amongst people.

Chapter 6, FROM THE HEART, describes the importance of being open-hearted.

Chapter 7, IMPRESSIONS OF PARTICIPANTS, consists of personal impressions of some of my course participants. They describe, each in their own way, how clowning influenced them and changed their attitude towards life.

## ↔ *Red* ↔

Red is the nose
of the clown
who makes you laugh.

Red is the colour
of love
which the clown gives you.

Red is the blood
that makes
the clown flow
from head to toe.

Red are your cheeks
when the clown
makes you blush.

Red is the heart
a heart of gold
the heart of a clown

*Jans*

# 1. The clown

*"The clown in you is that open-minded, impulsive part that small children possess naturally."* (1)

‘**t**he’ clown does not exist. As people come in many shapes and sizes, there are also many different types of clowns. They can be sad, shy, dominant, clumsy, romantic, tragicomic, grumpy and even vicious. Every teacher in clowning has his own vision and interpretation of a clown. As for myself, the starting point is that a clown experiences the world like a child does, a child that explores the world through its senses. A child discovers the world with astonishment and purity; at first unintentionally, and then gradually with more awareness and refinement. A child's intuition is completely developed and the same goes for a clown's. However, discovering rationally is new to them.

I see a clown as an explorer of the world: he is curious about what the world has to offer. He does not have expectations but instead constantly discovers new things. He is completely in the here and now and experiences every moment intensely, his senses wide open. A clown is amazed about the possibilities and impossibilities of people, materials and mechanisms, but also accepts everything as it is. Especially since everything is so new to him, he makes the most extraordinary discoveries. He has an eye for the smallest detail and he wants to explore further still. Because of that, he continues to amaze himself.

*"Clowns have an exceptional way of seeing things differently. By looking at the world as something completely new, every meeting of people or things is an amazing exploration for a clown. Amazement means that the familiar makes place for new experiences and invigorating ideas, lightened by a smile. Amazement releases new energy. By experiencing differently you can see differently and then act differently."* (2)

However... sometimes people are rather serious, reserved or even disapproving. A clown does not understand why these people avoid him or call him a weirdo. But he can also take the comment 'you are so weird' as a compliment. He particularly responds to the connotations and the feeling he gets from the speaker; more than to the content of the words. Like a young child that likes it when you say with a smile, 'I am going to eat you.' It is the game, the attention, and the contact the clown enjoys.

A clown approaches people with childlike openness. He wants to play, but has no way of knowing how people will react. Of course he expects to have fun together and from this point of departure he will say 'yes' to the audience, the surroundings, and the situation. But things can change in a split second and therefore he needs to stay alert; so that he can respond adequately to what is about to happen. If something unexpected happens, the clown wants to investigate how it happened. The audience will consider him brave, but he is just curious.

*"A clown considers the world one big marketplace with colourful stalls, each of which displaying all sorts of fascinating things." (1)*

The imagination of a clown is given free reign by his positive out-look on life. He tries, fails, tries and fails again. He never goes into defence, does not retreat or get cranky. Difficult situations stimulate his creativity. By investigating and trying new things, the most in-genious solutions arise. Alternatively failures happen, but he forgets them rather quickly because of his short-term memory. This way, everything stays new and challenging.
A clown is someone who differs from the norm and therefore many people find him a hilarious apparition. In any case, he is not a dull person; he is a colourful master in the art of life.

## ↦ *Nonconformist* ↤

*"A clown shocks his audience and his cheeky behaviour sets them thinking." (1)*

A clown is a nonconformist. He displays maladjusted behaviour, does things completely differently and disregards codes and agreements. Limitations and uniformity have no grip on him. He wants to play, dance, laugh, sing, jump, run, shout.
A clown intensely enjoys the freedom he has. He is not aware of the fact that this might be a privilege, or that he might someday lose this freedom. Yet this way of living frequently gets him into trouble. He is convinced that he does everything right and is surprised when people do not join him in his game. He constantly clashes with structures, rules, the law, norms, morals and traditions of society. This causes many people to feel ill at ease near a clown; his liberal behaviour can even raise annoyance and resistance. Others may call him mad or stupid. Unconsciously, however, he holds up a mirror to people, which shows them how limited or tenacious they sometimes are in their ways of thinking and acting.

*"A clown is unfamiliar with the world. His reactions to the world are utterly un-warranted, 'unnatural' and unexpected. He is afraid of things without reason, he cries when we think he might start laughing and he is completely indifferent to imminent danger. He is spontaneous and can say everything. Because a clown looks at our world differently, he frequently blunders. A clown also lives by other norms; conventions for acting decently and politely are different in his world. That is why he may sometimes rant and rave and blow off steam." (1)*

The word 'clown' is etymologically derived from the English 'clod', meaning literally 'a lump (of earth)'. A 'clodhopper' is a lout, a boor, associated with stupidity, rudeness, and careless upbringing.

The origin of the clown's red nose comes from the fact that people who drink too much sometimes get a red nose from the alcohol and start chatting and joking unreservedly. When someone is drunk he will sooner respond directly from his emotions and make clear how he feels about things. This openness often causes hilarious situations, resulting in the interpretation that drunk people are mad and sober people are sensible and intelligent.

A clown's eccentric clothing and his special make-up originate from his desire to make himself prettier. A clown loves exuberant, colourful costumes and fun accessories. He is a grotesque character, and thus his shoes are too big, his jacket and trousers are either too small or too long, and the colours are striking.

Because of his stubborn behaviour, a clown often gets himself into situations where he is forced to choose between two things. Will he help the man who is just about to fall off a ladder, or is he unable to resist his innate urge to first pick up a sweet that's lying in the streets? When it becomes clear that he made the wrong decision, it will get even worse. This tragicomic aspect makes people sympathise with him, because it is so recognisable. It is the tragedy of dilemma.

His ignorance and his clumsiness often manoeuvre him into tricky situations. He does not know how to get out of the pickle and because he is so clumsy things get even worse. Sometimes it gets so bad that he is overcome by despair. For instance, when he wants to help put out a big fire, he cannot think of anything but to blow very hard, which only fuels the fire more. When he is given something fragile, like a ladybug, he accidentally squeezes it a bit too hard. Or when someone has a painful bump, the clown tries to push it back inside. Others often don't appreciate his 'help', and that while he is so eager to do things right!

Charlie Chaplin is possibly the best example of such a tragicomic clown. As a vagrant he belongs to the lowest of social classes and when he tries to do good it is always met with suspicion. For instance, it is painful to see him try so hard to help a young lady cross a wet street without getting dirty: he takes off his jacket and places it over a pool of mud. Next, we see her wealthy husband walk by, who takes his lady into the car and drives off, splashing the tramp with mud. It makes us laugh, but at the same time we feel sorry for him, thinking, 'oh, poor man'.

*"A clown is the embodiment of inappropriateness, of all human failure. He is the virtuoso of clumsiness in the whole spectacle. He is the layabout, the good-for-nothing, the boor. He is the elephant in the china cabinet. He is the opposite of law and order. He lives on the fringes, he is an anarchist. Amusing, cheerful, childlike, naive, absurd, whimsical, eccentric, bizarre, cruel, irrational. He sees and makes the world topsy-turvy." (1)*

↦ *People person* ↤

A clown is a character who is in close contact with his surroundings. Despite the fact that he often does his own thing, he loves people very much and wants to interact with them. The people in the audience are his playmates. A clown wants to catch the audience's attention in everything he does. This is just like little children who need constant confirmation from their parents: 'Mummy, look! I can hop on one leg! Isn't it good? Look at me, mummy! Mummy, mummy, look!'
A clown experiences 'being alone' as a punishment. He comes alive when meeting others. He needs the attention, like a flower needs water and light, and the audience gives him that. His open attitude is inviting. He stands there, without a filter, and you just have to look at him to feel connected to him.

*"A clown is someone who moves you, who opens himself, who is vulnerable, who does not keep back how he experiences the world. A clown shows on the outside what lives on the inside." (1)*

A clown lets the audience know that it is okay for them to be the way they are. He is the messenger of positive energy and with his enthusiasm he tries to bring across his heart energy. He wants to defrost them, stimulate them, touch them, and make them laugh. He knows how to touch them merely by looking into their eyes. As a result, people often relax and show him their most beautiful smile. This is a special gift to him.

A clown enjoys being the centre of attention. He certainly feels that he is a welcome guest. In his openness lies the belief that there needs to be no fear and, because of that, his sense of humour comes out easily. By giving someone a beautiful, warm, or positive feeling, he contributes to a more positive environment. He teaches us to be open and to act from the heart. As a result, he fulfils his own desire to make people happy. Of course he is then labelled naïve, and obviously he will not succeed in making everybody happy. But every time he moves something within another's heart, he has done a good deed. A clown does not do that from a rational consciousness, but it is the result of the disarming way he treats people.

A clown does not judge; neither himself nor others. He has a natural understanding of the imperfections of human beings. Seeing a clown, people can laugh about their own shortcomings. Accepting yourself the way you are, that is the message. Like this, clowning can work in a healing way, both for the person who acts the clown, as well as for his audience.

*"A clown sees a world devoid of suspicion or mistrust. He views the world as guilelessly as a young child, a world of outgoing friendliness that seeks only friendliness in return. And instinctively we know it and gladly offer that friendliness. The funny*

*make-up and costume are a big part of it, of course, because they remove a clown from reality. He's not going to steal your wife, take your job, menace your children or cause you discomfort by being of another race or espousing a different creed. A clown is a political, social and economic neuter. We can abandon our insecurities, doubts and suspicions in his presence; he will not take advantage of our temporary emotional vulnerability. He will never let us down."* (3)

### ↛ *Magnifying* ↚

A clown is always clearly noticeable because his peculiarities are magnified. Whereas people usually try to hide their flaws, a clown puts them on display for everyone who wants to take a look. Has he got a large nose, short legs or very thin arms? A clown does not hide anything, but accepts them and shows everything in full glory. Better yet, he enlarges his nose, he makes his legs look even shorter with a pair of loose trousers and wears a short-sleeved jacket to accentuate his thin arms. Ladies and gentlemen, please take a look over here!
This also leads to a natural difference between reality and fantasy. The clown is an archetype, a fairy-tale figure, a theatrical act. The spectator feels safe, is able to distance himself because of the act and frequently feels superior to the clown. Fantasy versus reality.

*"Someone in the audience makes a remark on the clown's terribly fat belly – which troubles him very much in real life and which he fruitlessly tries to get rid of. However, as a clown he will make it even bigger than it already is and compare it to other bellies in the audience. He is then disappointed to discover that a pregnant woman's belly is even bigger than his."* (4)

The process of magnifying also applies to the clown's inner life, to his emotions and his thoughts. He shows people around him what is going on inside of him; he is like an open book and has no secrets. A clown does what a child already does automatically: he displays his feelings without any reservations and because he exaggerates them it is impossible for others not to understand how he is doing. His grief is real grief and his happiness is visible from head to toe. As a spectator you know what you can expect from him. Through his game people become able to recognise their own inhibitions and insecurities.

## ↔ *A clown says 'yes!'* ↤

A clown accepts circumstances and matters as they are, he says 'yes' to what is. He does not try to change them, but at the same time he does more than just get through them passively: he plays with them. It is an active form of acceptance. He expresses whatever a certain circumstance triggers in him which, again, causes a reaction, and so on. He is curious why things are the way they are and he will often set out for field research. A ball of paper is not just a ball of paper. A clown can also create figures with it, or consider it a football and kick it. This way, he does not reject the ball of paper; he plays with it. He can be pleasantly surprised when a passerby makes him the gift of an empty plastic bag, because it has so much potential! He can be happy when it rains because it feels so nice on his head. When it is cold he will not be grumpy; instead he will search for inventive ways to fight the cold. He does that by finding warmth with other people (crawling beneath someone else's coat), by standing close to a lamp, or by dancing wildly. That way, he makes himself happy again. For a spectator this may seem quite silly, but you could ask yourself who is more clever: the person who opposes the cold and complains about it, or the clown who resigns to the cold and then plays with it? You can't change the weather, but you can change the way you deal with it.

To me, therefore, a clown is the king of tolerance. Tolerance means not going into defense, but accepting and dealing with the feeling that arises, even if it is less pleasant. Imagine a clown tripping and falling flat onto his face. First, he bears it and feels what it does to him. Perhaps he becomes angry or upset. For a moment he thinks about the emotions he encounters and embraces them wholeheartedly ('yes, that hurt!'). He accepts them as they are and shares them openly with the audience. This creates room inside of him that enables him to move on feeling 'empty' and refreshed. Moreover, when he is being laughed at or made a fool of, he usually does not see that as a personal attack. He has no ego, he knows no power struggles, and is therefore not easily hurt. So he just joins in laughing.

*"A clown cannot do without contact; he always says 'yes'. First to himself, then to others. For if you do not say 'yes' to yourself, others will not do so either. Saying 'yes' is knowing yourself, including all your qualities and flaws. A clown is a perfect example of someone who knows his own faults and flaws and looks at them with a laugh and a tear." (1)*

Let me give you an example of a situation in which I, as a clown, had a lot to bear. One Sunday morning I had a performance at a shopping mall. I left the dressing room full of energy and walked towards a woman and her grownup daughter. When the daughter saw me coming she shouted at me, very loudly, 'I really don't feel like this right now!' I instantly wanted to go back to the dressing room. Maybe this woman was having a bad day, or she felt threatened, or maybe she just disliked clowns. As a person I found it very difficult to let her just feel the way she felt and stay in my element. As a clown I could accept it more easily. For a brief moment I felt the pain of rejection, but then I politely said my goodbyes and walked on, searching for new encounters.

A clown is only disappointed for a short time. When something does not work out, he will just keep on trying. Again, and yet again. When it still does not work out, he will try it in a different way. Or he just lets go of his intentions and continues with new ideas and games in which he can be totally absorbed. All actions start from his extremely positive attitude towards life. Thanks to his perpetual energy, he constantly keeps himself going. To us that may seem very enervating, but to him it is natural.

Accepting that things go the way they go; it is as simple as that. You could almost call it a Buddhist lifestyle, an enviable attitude towards life. Personally, clowning has given me very beautiful things. I experience time and time again that saying 'yes' helps me accept difficult situations more easily. When I initially say 'yes' in my head, things instantly do not seem so bad after all. Am I stuck in traffic? I cannot change that. When something like this happens, I look around with curiosity, at the landscape, the sky and the people in their cars. Do I stand in a long queue in the super market? Annoying, but dramatic? My attention is directed at the customers, the cash girl and at the products that people have gathered in their shopping trolleys. Do I encounter an annoying colleague or a difficult course member? I try not get irritated, but accept that this is the way he is and see what I can learn from him. I try to let go of my judgements and prejudices, which gives me more peace of mind and satisfaction.

Of course I do not always entirely succeed at this.

↔ ↤

First, a clown says 'yes' to himself
*acceptation*
Then he can say 'yes' to others
*connection*
After that everything will start flowing
*energy*
Straight from the heart
*happiness*

↔ ↤

## ↦ *Letting go* ↤

Life is a continuous flux of getting to know someone or something, staying in touch, and finally letting go. Think, for instance, of a child on its own, without its father and mother (but with a babysitter) for the first time. A child taking its first steps (by trial and error). A child learning how to ride a bike without training wheels; going to primary school for the first time; travelling to secondary school all alone; leaving the parental home; and so on. The exact same goes for the parents. They are encouraged to let their children go and stimulate their independence.

When my children were little, I used to play a game with them of which I only later realised its significance. They would jump down from halfway up the stairs, straight into my arms. They jumped one step higher each time. This game taught them that letting go goes hand in hand with trust.

The improvising clown finds himself in a void; he has absolutely no idea of what is going to happen. When improvising, a clown relies on his feelings. He reacts like a child to whatever may come, full of optimism. Everything will turn out fine. The person behind the clown may not find that complete surrender natural. We were taught a long time ago not to act on our impulses; we think about our every action. The challenge is not to think too long about consequences and to act more impulsively.

For instance, in the middle of one of my performances I felt a strong urge to knock over my suitcase, which was filled with hundreds of small objects. Should I do it? Is it actually funny when I do it...? And how do I tidy it up later? It was a fight between reason and emotion, between head and guts. What could happen to me if I let go of everything and just act on my impulses? Finally, I did it and it felt liberating to knock it over. The audience responded so well to this spontaneous action that it enabled me to improvise even further. Afterwards, everyone helped putting the things back into the suitcase. My courage was rewarded.

A televised documentary on Pablo Picasso had made a huge impression on me. The painter was shown working on a portrait. When he had finished he took a few steps back and looked at it with deep concentration. Then he took up his brush, dipped it in a lot of paint and painted over the old portrait to create a new version. I couldn't believe my eyes! I had really liked that first painting. Why didn't he just put it aside and start on a new canvas? He could have asked a lot of money with that first and lovely portrait. Subsequently he created a new and magnificent piece of art. 'Leave it as it is', I remember thinking. But no, just like the first time, the master was not satisfied and added a thick new layer of paint. Afterwards I understood that creativity is inextricably linked to letting go, which is what makes an artist an artist.

As a human being it is impossible to completely let go of your thoughts. None of us will easily let go of control, because we are all too aware of the consequences of our actions. A clown, on the other hand, gets to act on his impulses, and do things at the spur of the moment. He does not think about whether things are allowed, morally acceptable or principled. He does not think, he acts. Sometimes he will fail, but he will do it openly. A clown has no inner critic who constantly looks over his shoulder to see whether his actions are okay. He is completely himself, playing from purity. A beautiful state of being.

*"A clown doesn't think, he acts. He goes straight for his target with confidence, curiosity, openness, alertness, and without being hindered by knowledge. Of course, naive as he is, he often trips, he fails... But he bears it in front of everybody, he gets on his feet and moves on cheerfully. That feels great!"* (1)

*↦ The clown as teacher ↤*

To me a clown has fifteen remarkable talents. He:

1. has a cheerful outlook on life
2. intensely enjoys everything this world has to offer
3. always is himself
4. lives life the way it is
5. acts on his impulses
6. is allowed to make mistakes
7. is sure of the things he does
8. is a star at showing his emotions
9. shows enthusiasm without inhibitions
10. is able to bear disappointments
11. keeps trying after failures
12. looks for contact with everyone
13. has faith in the goodness of people
14. doesn't judge others
15. shows his love without reservation

Through my experiences as a clown I learned to communicate better as a person and to say what I really want to say. What bothers me, what makes me happy, what touches me. The openheartedness of a clown, his creativity, and his (unconscious) courage help me realise how I lead my life, where I encounter difficulties, and how I can deal with these difficulties. I can get to know myself better through dialogue with others and by continuing to communicate in an open manner. I discovered the value of accepting the unexpected and I am able to enjoy new developments more. Not having or wanting to be in control all the time feels liberating. I do not have to look back at the past anymore and I can become more aware of my presence in the here and now. When there are no expectations beforehand, there can be no disappointments afterwards. Because of this, I now have a more relaxed outlook on life. It is actually quite extraordinary that the unstable and emotional character of the clown made me a more balanced person.

# 2. What type of clown are you?

Hair

Eyebrow

Face
Cheeks
Nose

Mouth

Shirt

Tie

Adornment 1

Adornment 2

Coat

Trousers

Suitcase

Socks

Shoes

Ton

Niederlande

Hair — curly, with gel on both sides, pointing outwards as though these are two wings.

Eyebrows — light brown, and above them white half circles with a light brown outline.

Face — light brown makeup as foundation.

Cheeks — cheeks red from rouge, which makes me look kinder.

Nose — red circle applied with face paint and outlined with a thin black line.

Mouth — only the lower lip painted red, curling upward. Around it a few white lines.

Shirt — light blue and not ironed (he is not the ironing type).

Tie — somewhat too short and in my favourite colour, yellow.

Adornment 1 — a toilet freshener with plastic flowers in it. Before my performance these are sprayed with an extremely sweet perfume.

Adornment 2 — a picture of myself in a small, golden, heart-shaped frame.

Coat — warm, woollen, checked coat. In the inside pocket there are pictures of myself to hand out.

Trousers — a pair of faded green corduroy trousers.

Suitcase — almost falls apart because of its weight, but I just can't say goodbye to it. In it there is an enormous amount of useless little things I picked up during my travels.

Socks — red (in order to be more down to earth).

Shoes — heavy army boots with hard toe caps.

*"A clown...is! You cannot act being a clown, you are a clown. A clown is a way of being, almost a philosophy. There are no types of clown. In every person lurks a clown, your own, authentic clown."* (1)

*i* will start this chapter with an introduction of myself as clown and all the aspects that have made him the way he is. I write about him in third person; he is a character I feel connected to but whom I can also observe from a distance. What drives my clown and what typical characteristics does he have? In providing you with this information, I invite you to search for the clown that is hiding within you.

↔ *My clown* ↤

I perform solo every now and then and I wander around with my suitcase hoping to make a loving connection with people. My clown does not have a schedule, no standard sketches, only one trick, and hardly any attributes. However, he does have a warm heart.

My clown wants nothing but good encounters; the more the better. He appeals to people's emotions. He enjoys most things that spontaneously arise within him: surprising silliness, itching impulses. He takes the responses he gets from people into his game. Which mimics or actions spellbind them? What is it they laugh about?

He does not want to distinguish between people, but sometimes that is inevitable. Then he zooms in on a woman wearing eye-catching and colourful clothes. Or he looks at the boy with the thick purple quiff. And at that girl who looks so sweet and has a wonderful smile. He just has to wink at her.

My clown wants to see and discover more about all the things he enjoys. He loves it when he moves his audience. The look in his eyes is often experienced as very intense and whenever he shows his helpless, endearing face, he gets reactions such as, 'oh, I would love to take you home!' or 'can I help you with something?' or 'would you like a sweet, an ice cream, or a glass of lemonade?'

My clown looks around himself like a curious traveller with an eager, though slouching posture. He does not use words but expresses himself through mime. In this way he is able to express his feelings better. His amazed eyes look at you questioningly as if he wants to say, 'I just don't know anymore, could you please help me?' His look is innocent like the endearing baby face of Harry Langdon, mixed with the straight-faced and stoic expression that characterized Buster Keaton.

*Harry Langdon*          *Buster Keaton*

His suitcase is filled with all kinds of things: toothbrushes, toys, sweets, and a lot of things he either found or was given. It makes his suitcase even heavier than it already was. However, for some reason he likes walking around with such a heavy suitcase. When they ask, 'What is in there?' (and people ask that very often), he only shakes the suitcase so that it makes a lot of noise. That in itself people find funny. Or he lets someone lift the suitcase. Most of the time, that person is shocked by its weight. Only few people get to take a glance inside the mysterious suitcase. Whenever that happens, either a scream or laughter escapes from his or her lips: amazed to find so much rubbish…

Frequently, my clown sits or stands very close to somebody in the audience and because he appears quite harmless, most of the time he is allowed to do this. He knows just as little as anyone else about what is going to happen. That causes tension for both sides and is therefore exciting at the same time. Who is going to do something? How will the other respond to that? What does the audience think of it? Of course, he is looking for 'the smile'. He is aware of the fact that the people around him are laughing and he likes that. But what exactly is the reason?

Often, he decides to sit quietly on his suitcase and watch people around him move. He enjoys the parade of passersby; he does not know where to look first. Sometimes people are startled as they did not notice him in the crowd. Suddenly he sits there, right in front of them, with his big, expressive eyes. People stick around a little, expecting something to happen. Apparently, typical expectations linked to clowns include extravagance and show. But this clown does not seem to do anything but watch. They do not understand that inside, my clown is working very hard to make something happen. He is a little disappointed when someone asks, 'at what time are you going to start, Mister Clown?' He feels as if he is not seen for what he is. This is me! But hey, people like to have something to hold on to; they want to know what they can expect. With this clown, you do not know this, but he looks sweet and makes a safe impression. Especially because people can literally look down on him when he is seated on his suitcase. Moreover, he looks so harmless, that people often accept his invitation to come and sit beside him on the suitcase. They are obviously excited since they do not control the situation. Suddenly they have become part of the play. My clown enjoys this and at the same time he finds it perhaps just as exciting as his visitors. He hopes that something arises that is enjoyable for both of them as well as for the people who are watching.

Time flies when my clown is having fun. Sometimes he performs for two hours without a break. But at the same time, it is exhausting too, because he tries to pay attention to every single person crossing his path. He is always alert, makes quick and intense eye contact and thus exchanges a large amount of non-verbal information. This contact comes straight from the heart and is not stopped instantly when he loses sight of this passerby. Sometimes, he follows him or her with his eyes for minutes. He calls it an 'encounter of the soul', at least this is how he experiences it. A short exchange of feelings and openness. This makes my clown deeply joyful.

The biggest compliment my clown can get after a performance is that he is a 'human' clown. That behind the clown, you can see an actual person made of flesh and blood with whom you can communicate pleasantly. That there is interaction where both can have fun. And, most of all, that you are allowed to enjoy safely from a distance. There is something magical about the short encounter with this clown, indefinable, yet friendly and warm.

## ↔ *A Wandering Heart* ↔

I am the clown who wanders
into the eyes of the people
whom I meet.

I see, hear, and feel their stories
leaf briefly through their lives
fold dog-ears.

I am the clown you can confide in
without having to speak a word
for a second, let's look
deeply into each other's eyes
and understand profoundly.

As a reward I offer you my heart
unconditionally and to you alone
hello person, I do not know you
but I like you
you are unique.

Being yourself is the most beautiful thing there is.

Show me your most playful smile
then I will treat you to
my most childlike innocence.

*Ton*

## ↪ *Where did my clown come from?* ↩

In 1969, I was a ten-year-old who regularly watched German television. They broadcast a comedy series named 'The Comedy Capers'. These were old black-and-white films about silly characters who constantly caused trouble. Police officers with spinning clubs tried to catch them but the protagonists always somehow thought of something that could save them. I identified very well with these underdogs who turned out to have names as: Harold Lloyd, Charlie Chaplin, Laurel and Hardy, Buster Keaton and Harry Langdon. The children's faces of 'Our Gang' are still engraved in my memory.

Back then, I knew little about clowns, and the ones I did know from television I did not like at all. However, the abovementioned comedians touched something in me that became the foundation of my future profession as a clown. I only realised a lot later how much I had actually learned about humour and timing by watching these funny guys on a weekly basis.

When I was about twenty years old, I signed up for acting classes in my hometown, Tegelen. Soon I discovered that I was not born to be an actor. I was not at all able to feel and play a character. I admired people who could let themselves go completely and entirely dive into a role. I wanted to be like that, but how?

Then our theatre group was offered a clowning course, taught by a guest teacher. I found this course to be very exciting, and I also felt the immense energy clowning gave me.

I will never forget how one evening I was asked to show my twenty silliest walks to the rest of the group. I was the last one in the group and I had already seen about two hundred walks. I felt fear... Would I be able to think of something original? I completely froze up until I said to myself, 'Come on, get out of your head and dive into your energy!' I put myself into motion and from played enthusiasm I tried some silly steps. Soon I got into a buzz and I started to enjoy what my body conjured up. I also enjoyed the cheering and laughter from the audience. Suddenly, there were no worries anymore about whether it would be a success or not. I was no longer in the area of failing or succeeding. I cannot remember what I exactly did, but I do know that it was a moment of enjoyment free from worry. Years later, I was able to describe this state of mind as; 'losing yourself in something', 'emptying your head' or 'getting into a flow'. A student of mine later described such an experience with the profound words, 'I just happened!'

In 1982 I met Frans Custers. We got to know each other in a men's club, where men came together to discuss what it meant to be a man and your place as a man in society. Next to discussions, there was also room for theatre and cabaret. Together with Frans and two other guys I founded a cabaret group for men. We sang songs about male eman-cipation and about the questions we as men (well, as boys, rather) had about that issue. After having practised for a few months, we decided we wanted to do something entirely different. The idea came up to buy some silly objects, put them in a suitcase, and walk among the crowd as clowns at a carnival celebration. Everyone agreed. However, on the day of the carnival, the other two men cancelled unexpectedly, which left Frans and me on our own. Despite our nerves, we dove into the adventure. To our surprise, we did really well. We both immensely enjoyed performing together with people. We discovered the magic of improvising, acting in the moment. *Duo Het Elftal* was born and we were determined to continue.

During the first two years we mainly performed for children. However, we both thought this target group was too restless and that it did not fit with what we had in mind. We wanted to improvise from a state of attention and tranquillity. We preferred an adult audience with whom we could have fun on a more subtle level. This sudden twist was partly

*Duo Het Elftal*

due to a course we attended where we were introduced to another way of clowning: modest, refined and... non verbal. We both loved to do this and our clowns changed from extrovert to introvert. We decided to walk hand in hand, as two friends; we were very quiet and looked around in amazement. Frans, being the short one, walked in front of me carrying a large suitcase. Me, being the tall one, trudged behind him carrying a small suitcase. The idea was to get a response from the audience by looking silly (though attentive) and after that improvise with their reactions. Throughout this all we had Keatonesque poker faces, reflecting only the slightest amazement. Amazement brought about by that intriguing human behaviour. During the course of our performances, more and more did I manage to let go of my thoughts and again I felt the power of improvising. I was also able to trust the fact that things will always work out in the end; alone, with the help of your buddy, or together with the audience.

At the end of the 80s, when I was thirty, I officially clowned for a living (I always found it very special to be able to fill this in on official documents...). Frans and I had gradually grown towards this and now we were official artists who travelled through the country and abroad. It was great to receive so much appreciation for our clowning skills. I am convinced that our success was also due to the fact that we were sweet, male clowns; we were men who, through their clowns, showed their tenderness and vulnerability. We saw and heard that this touched many people.

In 1991, *Duo Het Elftal* stopped performing, and together with Annet van Zeijst I formed *Duo Biek*. Same idea, same form of clowning, but this time with a woman as my partner. I discovered that it was totally different to perform with a woman. Femininity, sensitiveness and communality were aspects that sometimes clashed with my own clown, but they also enriched him. And, of course, myself as well. I performed with Annet until 2003, after that I played solo.

*Duo Biek*

## ↔ My clown and I ↔

Looking back, it can't have been a coincidence that I got involved in the world of clowning. As a clown, you are free; you can be the playing child and you do not judge yourself or others. You can openly show your love for people. And in that clown I recognised the same outsider feeling that I recognised in myself. I was no follower who wanted to be part of a group; I wanted to make contact out of my own initiative. I strongly desired the freedom to do whatever I wanted; to be free from what others wanted. The clown felt as I felt myself: rebel, anti-hero, and romantic in one.

My clown and my ordinary self don't act always the same, although that is my deepest longing.

The clown I play is the human Ton
whom I passionately long for

I want to learn how to give and receive love wholeheartedly
and be in utter agreement with myself
so I can be child again.

I envy his freedom, shamelessness and his absence of fear. I want to celebrate life just as spontaneously as he does, childish and without prejudices. As a clown I easily approach people I would normally avoid. My rational thoughts, informing me about the possible consequences of a risky encounter, sometimes send me in another direction. The more experience I have in performing, the less flexible my clown becomes. I have accumulated so many experiences that it becomes harder and harder to empty my head over and over again, and to perform with the naivety that comes from the basic assumption that 'everything is new'. However, my clown is more mature, and more free to make something happen without having to respond immediately.

It's great to see how my clown and I developed simultaneously. I need less and less (attributes) and take less and less action; it's enough just to be there. Because everything is there already!
The choice to work this way has brought me lots of good fortune. I used to be too rational. For years I worked as a clerk, since I liked being in control and because I enjoyed organising things. Getting in touch with clowning invited me to take risks. It became a real challenge not to lose my balance when unexpected things happened.

I personally experienced how hard it can be to find out which type of clown suits you best. After my first clowning duo, *Duo Het Elftal*, was finished, I desperately searched for an entirely different type of clown. I wanted to distance myself from that first clown and start playing a completely new character. I primarily focussed at appearances and at some point hit rock bottom when I played a drunken clown. The solution presented itself when I had become so desperate that I decided to visit one of my first teachers, Jan Rauh. He asked me a very powerful question: 'Why do you want to distance yourself from the aspects that actually made your former clown so good?' I considered this to be a real eye-opener. The romance could stay, as well as my clumsiness and ignorance. In addition, I started taking lead and I showed more of my masculine side in relation to my female partner Annet. Moreover, I dared to show my vulnerability more. By somewhat shifting the emphasis, I discovered my new clown step by step, and yet I remained true to myself. This way, it became more and more obvious which other aspects there were to my clown.

*"Clowns are a crossing between a poet and an orang-utan. Only sensitive men and women can let that come across credibly."* (1)

## ↔ *Which clown is inside of you?* ↔

My clown is a composition of the following qualities: curious, soft, open, sensitive, warm-hearted, romantic, and playful. In the courses I give in clowning, I help the participants in their search for the clown that suits them best. What qualities do you possess? What are your strengths? What kind of positive things do others say about you? As soon as you magnify these qualities and then make them a part of your clown, you show something of yourself which is essentially authentic. It is recognisable to others, which gives them something to hold on to. Actually this way is the easiest way: you do not have to make anything up and you can remain yourself. A clown is not just an actor that takes on an external role. The person behind the clown needs to remain visible in order to truly connect to the audience.

When answering the question, 'what qualities do you possess?', do not think of practical skills such as playing the piano well, being able to paint wonderfully or being tremendously good at football. It is about the intrinsic values of your personality.

I think the main quality of my clown is that he wants to radiate love and share it with people around him. His (my) curiosity is part of it, in the sense that if you love people, you are also interested in them. One way to find out which characteristics are central in the clown you play is by choosing one or more qualities (see page 51) and adding the word *too* to it. For instance: *too* energetic, *too* polite or *too* kind-hearted. As a clown, you show this in all its splendour.

Imagine that you are a sensitive person. Magnifying this automatically leads to hypersensitivity. Should you be too helpful, this can lead to meddlesomeness. And when you start to exaggerate your self-confidence, arrogance lurks around the corner. Over-exaggerating your qualities can become your nemesis in ordinary life: overanxious, oversensitive, overconfident. These are all characteristics you or the people around you may find bothersome, but as a clown you show this with pleasure. All these qualities are aspects of yourself. By strengthening them and consequently revealing them, you can make space for self-reflection and putting things into perspective. The clown turns his weaknesses into a comedy and accepts his flaws.

*"As a clown you can be more open and more foolish; you do not have to understand anything. In everyday life you have to be well-organised. If you are a scatterbrain and prefer not to show this, your clown can do so. You even exaggerate a bit and people like it." (1)*

How do you find out what your qualities are? It is hard to do this alone without ending up navel-gazing. Help from someone who can mirror you is very supportive. Ask a person you trust to exchange thoughts about this. Does the other perceive you in the same way you perceive yourself? Take plenty of time and write down a number of qualities. Then put the word *too* in front of them. Find out which qualities make you feel good.

The key to becoming your clown does not necessarily have to be a positive *quality*, but it can also be a typical *characteristic*, which is so like you that it is easy to act out. For instance, my clumsiness, naughtiness and naivety are typically me (though the last characteristic could also be regarded as a quality). They are not the main traits of my clown, but they are a substantial part of him. Other characteristics could be, for example, arrogance, brutality, dreaminess, lankiness or quick-temperedness. Try to act out several characteristics and play with them. It is better not to pick characteristics that are too modest to act out well. Think, for example, of acting patient, quiet, or expectant. A clown does not know what to do with these characteristics, because he is too outwardly focussed. So if you choose to be a shy clown, you must be able to act out his shyness.
Qualities are for example:

· sensitive ·
· trustworthy ·
· cheerful ·
· helpful ·
· spontaneous ·
· patient ·
· brave ·
· creative ·
· down to earth ·
· curious ·
· romantic ·
· social ·

· precise ·
· headstrong ·
· humorous ·
· playful ·
· flexible ·
· goal-oriented ·
· honest ·
· caring ·
· optimistic ·
· self-confident ·
· understanding ·
· intuitive ·

· energetic ·
· adventurous ·
· soft ·
· polite ·
· sweet ·
· relaxed ·
· resolute ·
· responsible ·
· passionate ·
· grateful ·
· kind-hearted ·
· loving ·

Of course, a clown is not one-dimensional, and neither is a human being. That would be too easy. Try to find out which different qualities and characteristics your clown has.

The following exercises might help to gain a better insight into yourself and into which aspects are useful while searching for your type of clown. When do you find a connection, and which characteristics might be interesting to investigate further? Try to remain honest, so that purity and transparency are present. At the same time, do not forget to put things into perspective, in order to prevent them from becoming too serious.

### Exercise 1: In memoriam

*Goal:* to gain better insight into who you are.

During this first exercise, you are going to look at yourself through the eyes of someone else, namely a person who knows you very well. This can be your husband or wife, your best friend, but not one of your children, because this relationship is unequal and it might conjure up too many emotions. From the perspective of this person, write your own 'In memoriam'.

Imagine the following situation: you have just died, at this age, in this phase of your life. Write down on a small piece of paper, a short funeral oration in an ironic way. Of course there will be sadness about your sudden passing away, but that is not up for discussion right now. You will look at the space that has become available now that the other one is released from your typical character traits, your annoying habits and distinctive ways. All this does not have to be devoid of love; on the contrary, it should be honest. I will give an example of one of my participants; Monica writes from the perspective of her lover John.

Dear Monica,

So now you are not here anymore. What peace and quiet! Never again a house filled with paint and paintings, in bright colour combinations that disrupt the tranquillity. You wanted to rest and have time for yourself, but I had to be present all the time.

No more of your chaotic way of cooking, working and cleaning within an hour and doing everything at the same time. Your hilarious enthusiasm for all the things in life you still wanted to do. And your whining and constant doubts about doing this or not, I won't miss them.

We'll never again play Rummikub, with your endless rearrangement of pieces, to eventually add no piece at all or one at the most.

No more long, exhausting bicycle rides through grasslands, which all looked the same to me, although you saw differences.

No more fixed plans for healthy salads in spring and summer and warm soups in winter.

No more dance evenings at 11 p.m. when I was thinking about going to bed.

Finally being able to spend money which you considered to be savings for 10 ideas that floated through your head.

No more camping trips with four blankets under a small mattress and three blankets around me and five blankets folded on the backseat of the car in case you got cold.

I will miss hearing about all the things you saw and felt, your reflections on situations, your analyses and additions to moments that are very ordinary to me.

So, now I think I'll get a nice pizza for myself and eat it in front of the television. I will watch sports with the dog lying next to me on the couch. Without a blanket.

Goodbye dear Monica, rest in peace. You really deserve it.

John

This exercise will only succeed if it is written in a slightly ironic way and as long as you do not take yourself too seriously. After all, we are not *that* important or irreplaceable, are we?

Take ten minutes at the most to write down a short text on a piece of paper. It should not, in any case, become longer than one page.

When you are done, the time has come to read the text out to someone:

1. Put on some headgear, preferably a black (top) hat.
2. In one hand you hold your note, in the other one a little flower or twig.
3. Read the text aloud, in a neutral manner. Do not act; the words speak for themselves. While reading, try to maintain eye contact with your listener(s).

*Note:* Afterwards, do not go too much into personal details. It is more important to find out what showed most: your tendency to stay in control, your life spirit, your talent to connect people, your chaotic way of living, your need to take care, and so on. Try to find out which elements you find pleasant and easy to play so you can make them part of your clown.

---

## Exercise 2: Hey clown, what are you doing here?!

*Goal:* to discover and develop your qualities through non-verbal games.

In this exercise you will playfully discover and experience what makes your energy flow, and what affects you less or maybe not at all. The assumption is that you are a clown performing in the street. Your clown does not speak! A passerby approaches you.

1. Take a chair and sit on it, wearing your clown's nose. You play a clown who sits on his suitcase in the street, waiting for passersby.

2. Your partner plays a passerby (so without a nose) who suddenly sees you and starts to ask all kinds of curious questions. 'Hello, good to see you. Are you going to perform? Are you alone here? Do you get paid for this? Are you having a good time? Why are you wearing that silly hat?'

3. When you respond through mime, try to do this clearly: it is either yes or no. You act also very energetically, looking the passerby straight in the eyes. Try not to end up in the grey zone by shrugging your shoulders in a 'I don't know' kind of way—it slows down the energy and you risk losing the passerby. Essentially, a clown is positive and he will answer mainly with a 'yes', but try to find the other, naughtier side as well. Now and then, respond unexpectedly or illogically, for instance by replying with 'no' when 'yes' is expected. This creates more fun than following the familiar way.

An example:

Passerby: 'Do you like sitting here?'
Clown: *shakes his head in denial.*
Passerby: 'Then why do you do it?'
Clown: *makes a gesture of earning money.*
Passerby: 'Ah, so you make money doing this!'
Clown: *shakes his head.*
Passerby: 'How do you earn your money then?'
Clown: *makes a gesture of eating an ice-cream.*
Passerby: 'But doesn't that cost you money?'
Clown: *looks at him questioningly: Does it?*

And so on.

4. Maintain this question-and-answer game for a while. Try to find out what your qualities are through the interaction with this passerby. Try to respond spontaneously. Also try to exercise more

influence by using your body (leaning forward, slumped, careless) and your facial expression (endearing, surprised, naive).

5. You can extend the game by starting a non-verbal conversation and by asking the passerby questions through signs and mimic, such as 'What are you doing here?' or 'Do you have that feeling too?' or 'How did you get that overcoat?' and so on.

*Reflection:*
+ Which qualities did you enjoy using?
+ Subsequently, discuss which responses did or did not come across well.
+ When did the passerby laugh and why?
+ What could you have done differently?

*Note:* Afterwards, let your partner react by telling you which qualities he recognised most clearly in your clown. Next, tell him what felt familiar to you as a clown and what did not. Finally, change roles. This way, you can also experience what it is like for the other person.

---

## Exercise 3: Hello, here I am!

*Goal:* to make yourself visible to others, all alone and exactly the way you are.

1. Agree with someone to be your audience. Go stand behind a door or screen and decide on one of your qualities or typical characteristics. Take some time to get a feeling for it.

2. Next, make your appearance without your nose, take some steps forward and say to your audience: 'Hello, I am ... (mention your name).'

3.  Return to the door or screen and put on your nose. Step forward again and magnify that one quality, without it becoming a parody. Try to act it out and play with it. For example, when you are curious, maybe you could take a peek from both sides of the screen.
4.  Walk towards the centre and take some time to attentively observe your audience. Then, take a giant leap forward and shout: 'tadaaaaa!'
5.  Take some time to enjoy the applause and finally return behind the door or screen. Then put off your nose.

*Reflection:* Discuss with your audience how it went. Ask them what they honestly thought about what they had just seen:

+  What fit or did not fit the image they had of you?
+  Were they perhaps 'touched' by you at certain moments?
+  What caused that?

*Note:* Next, try some other qualities and/or characteristics.

---

It would be great if you manage to extract one adjective that characterises your clown, after having done these exercises. An example: the sloppy clown, the oversensitive clown, the punctual clown, the bossy clown, the control-freak clown, the exuberant clown, and so on. You can also show this through a special way of talking (if you choose to talk) or clothing and attitude. Suppose your are very punctual (quality), then wear a railroad cap, move stiffly and speak in a formal clown-like way. Or, when you are very tall (outward quality), emphasise your length by wearing clothes that are too short.

Dare to show all of this in a grotesque manner: a clown walks, acts, and talks always differently than an 'ordinary' human being. However, the main ingredients are your own; you do not need to make them up. You are your clown's starting point.

It is essential to be at peace with who you are if you want to present your clown well. Accepting who you are, including all your shortcomings and specific qualities, provides freedom in life. You do not need to hide anything anymore, nor do you need to be influenced by what other people think. If you dare to be 'real', it will do your particular clown much good. Of course this is not easy, as it forces you to face obstacles. These obstacles have increased since the beginning of your life. In the next chapter, I will invite you to return to your childhood in order to find out where your clown is hiding.

*"Clowning is an art of living in which you continuously develop. Nothing is added; rather, you peel away layers of yourself. When you have finally peeled away all the layers that you created around yourself over the years, you end up with yourself, your essence." (1)*

# 3. Returning to the inner child

↔ *The Inner Child* ↔

Thank you, silent clown
for the language of your heart
which I follow blindly

which I get to know more and more
and which houses childlike truths.

I want to be my own centre
my own home
but I need you
to see myself.

Behind all that grease paint hides my face
beneath these silly clothes the uncomfortable body
and in my head shelters that cursed thinking .

Behind your red nose I feel safe
hidden like a child behind the curtain
who, now and then, takes an excited peek

longing for everything.

*Ton*

*"We grew up much too fast. We noticed that grown ups often looked down on play-ing. They considered it a form of idleness and a waste of time. We were encouraged to give up our childlike ways, to become more serious and to behave maturely and productively. We learned that working was a good thing and that playing was somehow unacceptable. We learned that there was something wrong if an adult played. However, the human need to play is strong. When we ignore that need, we feel that something is missing in life and we try to fill the void."* (5)

*a* clown is a *homo ludens*, a playing human, carefree, playful and trying out new things. Like this, he discovers the world. A clown reflects the playful child in several ways: by his spontaneous way of responding to surroundings, his way of approaching others, and his curiosity to discover things.

In this chapter, I will take you back to your childhood, which is at the source of who you essentially are. Or better, who you could be if you dared to take the freedom to show who is truly inside of you. Not to be afraid to step into the light, as Nelson Mandela once said, but show your authenticity. To get there, some patterns may need to be broken. Let go in order to grow.

The personality of a human being is mainly formed during the first three years of his life. This is the developmental period of consciousness and the way in which the world is experienced. A child is completely dependent and its perception is only in a first stage of development. It is important for a baby to feel that it is allowed to explore, whine and cry without being immediately rejected. A baby is emotionally vulnerable and susceptible to warmth and loving contact. It experiences a symbiotic togetherness with parents and environment, in which consciousness of identity is absent.

As they grow older, children become more and more aware of the fact that getting attention is sometimes based on conditions. Parents expect certain behaviour, which is linked to punishment or reward. Children are taught that they are not always allowed to be themselves and they often have to adapt to other people's wishes. Sometimes they are silenced, or worse, not given any attention at all. This can be painful after a period in which they used to get lots of attention, only because of their dependence.

At the age of approximately two years old, toddlers do not perceive themselves as individuals, but as part of a unity instead. For example, little children say things like, 'Peter did a good job, didn't he, mum?' In this case, he speaks about himself in the third person. The difference between 'I' and 'you' is the manifestation of an own ego starting to develop. The connection with the mother becomes less intense and the focus becomes more outward. However, the safety net of the parents being around remains essential. There are huge developments when it comes to voluntary movements, speech and social interaction. A toddler is expected to do things on his own more and more. Independence is encouraged, but that automatically results in less attention. This often causes frustration to a child; it is not yet able to walk its own path (while the need is strongly present) and remains dependent on its parents. This results in the embedment of a deep feeling of incapacity. Partly because of this, the child's natural behaviour is hindered.

*"When a human is born, the emotional mind, the emotional body, is completely healthy. Maybe around three or four years of age, the first wounds in the emotional body start to appear and get infected with emotional poison. (...) When something is wrong, they react and defend themselves, but then they just let go and turn their attention to the moment again, to play again, to explore and have fun again. Little children express what they feel and they are not afraid to love."* (6)

Jung once used the term 'the magical child'. By this he means the natural child within us that has innate qualities for creativity, development and self-realisation. Playing is essential for children, as playing sets them in motion. They learn by trial and error, step by step, and with the necessary aches and pains. A child's will to grow is immense, the will to develop through discoveries. Triumphs are celebrated exuberantly and disappointments are dealt with. Young children are curious and assertive. They examine and learn to connect things in order to understand the world. This makes them creative and it enlarges their world of experience. On top of that they can vent their emotions in their play, which leaves room for spontaneous reactions.

Spontaneity is one of a child's biggest qualities. A child has the natural ability to act impulsively and instinctively; doing before thinking. This is inextricably linked with life energy. Repressing this undermines the pleasure of living. The process of constantly adjusting to the parents' wishes keeps a child from finding its own path in becoming an independent individual.

*"Adjusting yourself to the needs of your parents often leads (though not always) to the development of the 'pretender', or what is often called 'the false self'. The human being develops an attitude that merely shows what he is expected to show and he is completely absorbed by what he is showing. The true self fails to develop and to differentiate, because we cannot live up to that. The child's integrity is hurt and as a result, the living, the spontaneous is cut off." (7)*

A child needs compliments in order to create a positive self image. When too much is forbidden, it is not capable of discovering on its own. In case of too much control from the outside as well as too much care, a child will not be able to develop fully. Frustrations will come up and they will create a breeding ground in the child's inner self. A lack of balance in the 'yes' and 'no' messages will lead to a painful everlasting struggle to be seen as an individual character. A child wants to be able to act freely without being judged constantly.

Children are honest without the intention to hurt anyone. They say things just the way they see them. The way something is perceived often depends on the intention or the tone with which something is said. When, in all innocence, a child points towards a man's fat belly or a woman's red face, those are observations made without a judgement. They are solely an expression of what is perceived. Sometimes, this goes hand in hand with a sincere amazement, which has to do with the child's new discovery. For example this joke: A mother is sitting in the bus with her child. The child says, 'What a big nose that man has!' His mum says, 'shush!', to which the child asks, 'Doesn't that man know that he has a big nose?'

Because we are adults, we are inclined to draw the attention of our children to their shortcomings. However, in their short lives, children have not yet had much of a chance to collect a lot of material for comparison, and we should not blame them for that. It is from our own world of experience that we approach them. Sometimes we want to overprotect them. In doing that, we take away much of their inner strength, and as a result they become less and less comfortable relying on their intuition and spontaneity.

*"Children are never in doubt. If parents and teachers guide them properly, they learn to rely on themselves. People who are self-confident take wholehearted decisions. When children are exposed to rejection and disapproval, things go wrong. Parents who criticise their children too much, encourage them to be 'inside their own heads' and lose touch with themselves."* (8)

As we grow older, we recognise more and more how much we have been restricted. Sooner or later, the desire for the freedom of our childhood re-emerges. We gain more insight into who we are and what it is in this life that enables us to keep growing. We all seek confirmation, or at least some acknowledgement of our right to exist. Every person, young or old, wants to be seen, as they truly are. When this does not happen, or not enough, something essential within ourselves is touched and we feel hurt. Our hurt child can ask or even scream for attention, but it can also deal with the pain in silence, for fear of losing the love of others, especially its parents. In other words, we have lost our confidence.

A clown can help us to revive parts of that trust by letting us experience what we felt in former times: warmth, safety and the joy of playing. A clown takes us back to the confidence we once had as a child. Everything seemed makeable and the world was one giant playground. It should be perfectly natural for adults to behave like a child.

## ↣ *My childhood* ↢

Despite the fact that it could be very pleasant at my parent's home, I mainly remember what my parents did or did not consider socially acceptable. For example, emotions could not be expressed freely. Being angry or arguing was effectively forbidden as we were only allowed to be nice to each other. Being abundantly happy was unnecessary and grief was something you did not show openly. The constant repression of these emotions resulted in me becoming more and more disconnected from my emotions. From primary school onwards, I lived rationally and thoughtfully, although I only managed to see that clearly afterwards. I did not approach life from an inner core that guided me - I used my head more than my gut feeling. I always felt uncomfortable when surrounded by other people. I admired some people for their authenticity and as a result started to imitate them.

Being the youngest of five boys, I know the feeling of not being seen, by neither my parents nor my brothers. Where other children might have expressed their discontent, I kept it shut inside. I was full of fear and insecurity and I did not feel as though I mattered. My elder brothers apparently knew everything better and they all led their own lives. They did not notice my strong need to share my perceptions.

I was unable to share when it came to music, sports, or other things that I felt enthusiastic about. On top of that I was easily influenced by atmospheres and moods while my brothers were (or seemed) so composed. I was different and I felt it.

I remember a situation that perhaps would mean nothing to other people, but that quite affected me. We were, as a family, sitting at the dinner table, and I was enthusiastically explaining something special that had happened at school. While I was telling my story, my mother asked, 'could you pass me the potatoes?' In the meantime, one of my brothers got up and walked off, and another one started to tell another story. 'Okay,' I thought, 'I will just keep my amazing stories to myself.' But in reality it felt as though someone was squeezing my throat.

Whenever I did not want to do something, my mother kept pushing until I finally decided to do it after all. If I didn't, I was a naughty boy. My boundaries were constantly violated and I felt invisible; I was judged by what I did instead of by who I was. Moreover, everything had to be perfect. This made me very insecure, and try my hardest not to fail. We were clearly told what was socially acceptable and what was not: hands above the table, chest out and mouth closed when chewing. My mother found it very important that our family appeared perfect to the outside world. When we had visitors, the house would be spick and span, we were dressed in our most beautiful clothes, our hair was combed well, and so on. Everything was done in order to make us look like a model family. I found this awfully oppressive and, on top of that, fake. My parents did not love me unconditionally; I had to earn their love. When I did exactly what was expected of me, things were fine. This felt suffocating, and it also burdened me with a feeling of guilt whenever I did things differently. I pleased and helped others, but I neglected my own needs. To me, it was normal to do things this way, as long as my parents (and everyone else) liked me.

*"A little child has to adjust to society which, in the beginning, does not reach beyond its own family. When he is disobedient, he is sent out of the room, in other words, disowned. This is very serious as it means losing love, and nothing is harder to cope with than that. The conflict that is going on here, repeats itself later on and continues for the rest of their lives; the clash between the wishes from the inside and the expectations of the outside world." (9)*

Because I kept adjusting myself to others, I hardly developed my identity. My ego was insufficiently nourished, which resulted in an extreme focus on the outside world. Linked to this was an immense feeling of guilt: 'When I don't do the right thing, I will fail towards others.' When I got older, I became very sensitive to criticism. When people did not respond enthusiastically enough to what I had to say, or when someone made a remark or gave criticism, I felt pain, over and over again. It felt as though I was rejected as a person, and for me it reinforced my conviction that I was not worthy of other people's attention. I wanted to be heard and seen, but as soon as that happened, I wanted to be anonymous again. In relation to the people around me, it became clearer and clearer that I had a problem with communicating openly. I repressed a lot of emotions and carried the necessary secrets with me.

*"Whenever someone is not able to connect to his true feelings, he creates a 'hole in the soul'. This results in a false identity. 'Being nice' is one of these false identities. A nice woman never shows anger or frustration. She is merely acting." (10)*

Obviously, making contact was my theme. The fact that I became a clown cannot be a coincidence. He invited me to come outside. In the beginning this primarily took place in front of children, in a rather exaggerated way. Along the way, when performing for adults, it became more refined. Like so many other people, I ended up with a profession where I need to sort out most. You teach what you need.

Retrospectively I was able to perceive the strict social conventions as limitations to my development. Nowadays I am getting better and better at looking back at my past without bitterness; my parents had passed on what they had received themselves, and they did this with the best intentions. It brought me interesting challenges to sort out, and that eventually made me who I am today. By experiencing the consequences of having difficulties making contact with other people, I now see how things can be different, and pass this on. This is also linked to my desire to stimulate my creativity and my imagination. I have a strong drive to investigate how things work and whether they can be done differently as well.

↦ *Discovering* ↤

*"The field of wonder and amazement is magical. It enables us to go beyond fighting, to an open field of opportunities. This can be seen clearly in children — masters of*

*discovery. When children learn there is no judgement; no right or wrong. It is one big discovery. A child does not ask for support whenever it grabs something. It is too busy discovering. It does not feel guilty when knocking over a glass of milk. All its attention is aimed at the flow of liquid. This is discovery."* (11)

To me, making discoveries goes hand in hand with a basic attitude of amazement, which you see in a clown when he enters the stage. What kind of place is this? There's so much stuff here! What are all these people doing here, anyway? A lot of questions, without judgement. First there is the observation, then the discovery. For instance, a clown sees a chair on the stage and tries to sit on it in as many ways as possible. 'Why doesn't he just sit on it?', the audience wonders. The answer is, we see a child at work that is not yet able to do this effortlessly. Most adults do not accept childlike behaviour because adult behaviour is the norm. 'Peter, sit on your chair properly, will you?' This is one of the reasons why children like clowns so much. In the adult clown, they recognise their own clumsiness, as well as the frustrating restrictions that come with their young age.

When children are playing games you often hear them talk to their toys. This behaviour stems from the fact that objects can be alive in a child's imagination. Personifying objects is called 'animism'. All objects (rocks, trees, pencils, clothes, dolls) have a soul. It may seem as though only children are able to ascribe souls to objects, but we do it quite often as well.

For example, you want to start your car, but the engine is unwilling as a result of last night's frost. You may exclaim, 'Are we going to drive or what?!' Later, your car sputters uphill, and you encourage it by saying, 'Come on, come on!' When the traffic lights stay red for a very long time, you shout, 'Will this last very long or are we going to marry first?!' Finally, after a long drive, you arrive at your place of destination. You appear to be very satisfied with your car, and say, 'Well done, boy!'. You might even give it a friendly pat on its bonnet.

A clown continuously 'talks' with his surroundings. He makes objects talk, cry, become angry, run, fly, and so on, using his imagination. And he often clashes with his attributes as though they have control over him. It is great to watch a clown play like this, but it is even better when you experience it yourself being a clown.

## Exercise 4: Everything is alive!

*Goal:* to stimulate your imagination and creativity.

1.  When you are alone at home, wear your clown's nose and walk through the living room. This might feel strange to you, but the red nose can help you with this exercise. It works for me, because something within me changes as soon as I wear it.
2.  Next, start looking around through the eyes of an imaginative child, and imagine all things to be living beings.
3.  For instance, walk towards the door and knock on it. This action can be followed up immediately with a remark spoken aloud, for example: 'Sorry, I hope this was not too painful.' Other examples:
    - You notice an open CD case and you ask, 'I hope there is no draught in here?'
    - You eat a sandwich and you say, 'well, there you go. Have fun in my stomach!'
    - You drop something on the floor and you say to the object, 'hush, mind the neighbours!'
4.  Take a lot of time for this exercise and afterwards write down your greatest animistic discoveries.

*Reflection:*
- Were you able to turn objects into living things using this technique?
- How did you feel about looking at certain objects differently?

÷ Did you manage to let go of all logic and surrender yourself to a childlike behaviour?

÷ What do you think might happen if you apply this technique during a performance?

*Note:* Do not forget to take a good look at our teachers: little children who are completely absorbed in their fantasy world. Try to apply 'animism' while performing and imagine a child's voice.

---

As a child, to what extent did you have the opportunity to experiment? Were you allowed to mess with paint, to soil your clothes and to make a mess? This was certainly not the case at my home. Neat clothing, belongings tidied up nicely and no crazy actions. Moreover, my mother had all sorts of anxieties, which kept me from taking risks. I constantly had to watch out that I did not fall or hurt myself. She was terrified of dogs and so I did not pet them. During a thunderstorm we had to unplug all electrical appliances (and she would lock herself in the bathroom) and when we were in the car, she would repeatedly shout, 'look out!' Fear is a bad foundation for discovering, because it holds you back from being in contact with other people, and it prevents flexibility in unfamiliar situations. It caused me to become a very careful person, who was in extreme need of security and structure.

*"Studies show that 80% of all the input we receive as kids is negative ('don't do this', 'that is bad', 'watch out', and so on). If we remember that a child is like a sponge and he or she receives and believes anything that is said to him or her, there can be little wonder why we end up in a society of people whose belief systems contain creeds such as 'I am not good enough', 'I don't deserve it', and 'I'll mess it up'." (12)*

Taking chances, colouring outside the lines, giving unexpected answers? When red pen markings show up frequently enough, people will (out of fear!) choose security. However, it is exactly the acceptance of our creativity that causes us to develop and not to become stuck in set patterns. Many huge historical discoveries only came about after dozens of failures. The moment of eureka often occurred by coincidence, after a seemingly endless process of trial and error. In our contemporary computer era, where the left brain (intellect, logic) reigns, even more of a creative right brain counterweight is necessary.

Mentally preparing a 'yes' makes room for experiencing new things, and gives you access to your imagination and creativity. During the workshops in clowning I give to businesspeople, I try to help participants experience how enriching a positive attitude can be for themselves as well as for their environment.

## Exercise 5: Saying 'yes'

*Goal:* to experience the effects of a positive attitude.

This exercise is meant to make you aware of the imagination and originality that is inside of you, which is often hidden to yourself and to the outside world. You will need a partner, and you are going to make up a story in which you play the lead. Beforehand, you programme a 'yes' in your attitude. In doing this, you actually give priority to your gut instincts rather than to your rationale. This way you make room for associations and learn to rely more on your intuition.

1.  First, your partner hands you an opening line such as, 'yesterday, I walked on the beach', or, 'yesterday, my grandma came to visit me', or, 'yesterday, I did some shopping in the supermarket'. This will be the first sentence of your amazing story.
2.  Now it is your turn to start talking. Repeat your partner's first sentence and continue talking from there. Make up as you go along.

3. After a few sentences your partner suggests a word that has absolutely nothing to do with the theme of your story. At this point, you mentally say 'yes' to this word, you accept it into your story. Everything you say thereafter will lead to your usage of this word, as though it were the most natural thing. Try not to fit in the word too quickly, but take your time. This will make your story more interesting to listen to.

4. When the word has been used in your story your partner can throw in a next word. He will continue suggesting new words as soon as you have integrated the previous word. It is most amusing if your partner throws in the strangest words to make it difficult for you. This will challenge your creativity. If your opening line is, 'yesterday, I walked through the forest', your partner should not suggest words such as fungus or pine tree; he should choose more challenging words, such as fridge, pneumatic drill, or cash dispenser.

5. Whenever your partner has trouble thinking of words to suggest, a possible solution could be for him to not listen too attentively to your story. He should concentrate on finding words, since that is an important factor that makes this exercise a success. If he still cannot think of a word, he should look around. The room you are in contains more than enough words: carpet, lamp, painting, window, and so on. It is not very original but already much better than a long silence.

The longer the story, the crazier and more fun it becomes. After about five minutes you can switch roles.

*Reflection:*
+ Were you able to associate quickly?
+ Did you manage to let go of devising a logical plot?
+ Were you able to let go of the pressure to succeed?
+ Which part of your story did you like most?
+ Why?

*Note:* This exercise is a good metaphor for saying 'yes' to impulses that people provide when you are performing as a clown. Also it will help you to become more open in daily life.

---

When my son Steef, at the age of four, went for a trial at primary school, Miss Vera gave him a game board with coloured pencils. He got to work, but several minutes later, the teacher told him that *these* colours belonged in *this* place and *those* belonged over *there*. My son briefly looked at her and then stoically continued his own way.

*"During the development from childhood to adulthood, creativity diminishes. Researchers have looked at people's ability to generate original ideas. The number of original answers at the age of five is 90%. At the age of seven, this number has decreased to 20%, and many adults only succeed in giving 2% of original answers."* (13)

## Exercise 6: Discover, discover, discover!

*Goal:* to experience everything around you with childlike curiosity.

Make sure you are home alone so that you will not be disturbed. Take plenty of time for this; about fifteen minutes. If you are having a good time playing, time will fly.

1. Try putting yourself in the shoes of a toddler, between the age of one and two. You do not know what everything is meant for yet and you are on a quest.
2. Choose any object in your room and look at it with a lot of curiosity.
3. Try to do a lot of different things with this object. The challenge is to become entirely focused on discovering and investigating it. What can you do with a roll of tape? You can make sounds by

tapping on it, take a peek through the hole, make it spin like a wheel, and so on.

4. Use all your senses: how does your object feel, move, smell, taste? What sounds can it produce? Investigate and observe through sensory experience, not through your already present knowledge.

5. As soon as you begin to realise all too well what kind of object it is and what purpose it serves, let go of it and choose another toy.

*Reflection:*

+ Were you able to focus and disappear in your investigation?
+ Was it liberating to do or were you unable to let go of your thoughts?
+ Were you able to experience childlike astonishment and the sense of fun that comes with it?

---

Other challenges that help your discovery practice in daily life:

+ Take a different route to your workplace, to the city or to your friends. Even if it is a detour, find out what this new road has to offer. Pay full attention to it.
+ When you are visiting someone, curiously look at their books, CDs, paintings, and the overall decoration of the place. Everything provides you with information on the resident's world of experience.
+ Read books you would normally never read, listen to music you normally strongly dislike, watch unfamiliar television programmes. Try to find out whether there are elements you find interesting after all.
+ Turn to nature with all your senses. Observe leaves, branches, footprints, or whatever you may find.
+ Make small movements with your fingers and hands and let yourself be amazed by all the things they can do: how they move, how the

veins and muscles constantly change, what kinds of sounds you can produce with them, and so on. Take as much time as needed.

## Exercise 7: Create your own story

*Goal:* to make associations in order to enhance your creativity.

1. Take any book from your bookcase and point at a word with your eyes closed. As soon as you have found a noun, write it down on a piece of paper.
2. Pick nouns from other pages as well and as soon as you have five words, you can stop.
3. Now you are going to process these five words into a miraculous narrative in which you use your childlike imagination. Spread the nouns throughout the text and try to connect them within the story. Let the most unexpected things happen: for instance, a talking table, a hungry airplane or a lonely coffee bean. Include expressive descriptions, surprising turns, humour, and of course a lot of creativity.
4. Maybe you would like to read out your story to someone else.

*Reflection:*
+ The actions of a clown are often based on illogicality. Did you experience that it is this that creates humour?
+ Did you hold back, or could you have been even sillier?

*Note:* For example, get inspiration from the absurdity of Monty Python or cartoons likes Bugs Bunny.

Shame is a huge obstacle on the road to complete freedom. This feeling causes you to show modified behaviour and, at the same time, it makes you dependent on the judgment of others. Young children do not feel shame; they do things without having ulterior motives. When they want love and attention, they simply ask for it. For adults, shame has a social function, as we feel safer (read: less vulnerable) when our emotions are kept inside. We often do not dare to laugh freely or show our fears. We control our anger and we do not cry in the presence of others. In short, we are blocked.

A clown is free and he does not concern himself with the question of what others might think of him. There is no feeling of guilt and therefore he does not count on punishment. He is just a playing child.

*"Being a clown means nothing more and nothing less than being yourself. Daring to show your inner core without wondering what 'the other' might think of it."* (1)

When you are trying to let go of set patterns and familiar structures in daily life, you are inevitably faced with resistance. Fear of the unknown often causes people to choose security, even in unpleasant situations. Opposing change makes us become aware of our limits. It is a good thing to feel those limits and it is important to respect them. But when you accept new developments, you cease to ignore your deepest feelings, and you restore contact with yourself.

When working together with a particular colleague, I sometimes experience my limits very clearly. During his lessons he is very straightforward when commenting on something, and sometimes he uses swearwords. I find this highly enjoyable, because I see that it is pure and impulsive. Of course, as a child, I was never allowed to curse, and now I am sometimes lost for words as to how to put something.

My ratio remains in charge. But how liberating it is when, every now and then, I hear my thoughts spontaneously being voiced out loud. Fortunately, I am able to enjoy childlike behaviour more and more, that of others as well as my own. I experience it as purifying and healing when I completely let go of my thoughts and enjoy myself without a voice inside offering constant critique: 'Man, what on Earth are you doing?!' For instance, this happens at moments when I am dancing, performing, and teaching. When my inner critic is bothering me, I vigorously move my elbows back a few times and shout: 'Go away! Go away! Go away!' Good riddance.

*"Humans have a unique ability to split into two and both act and watch themselves act — and this division allows for reflexivity. But the sickness of excessive self-consciousness expresses itself in an inability to fuse the viewer and the viewed, an inability to engage in an activity and at the same time forget that you are doing this. There is a lingering sense of a mirror or a third eye, forever questioning, evaluating, or simply watching what the central self is doing." (14)*

↦ *Grief* ↤

Sometimes, the practice of clowning confronts you with things you have lacked in life. During my courses, some participants have unexpectedly been overcome by grief. Experiences from the past, which are supposed to be hidden unreachably far away, suddenly pop up again. It comes as a complete surprise, because all the old grief was thought to have vanished. But there are scars which have not yet healed entirely. Even though we do not remember exactly what happened in our youngest years, we often do remember the emotions that were linked to a specific event.

At one time, one of my participants had to cry because the freedom she experienced during her clown's act was overpowering. She was allowed to do all this without being frowned upon! It came as an epiphany that people even had to laugh, not at her but because of her.

I recognise the sadness of my course participants, the pain of the hurt child. The child that hid away and did not dare to openly show itself. Through physical exercises I try to help the participants connect to that pain in a loving way, and I show them that they are perfect just the way they are. By playing, participants get in better touch with their feelings. I invite them to follow their desires and not to hide their emotions. Everything they were not allowed to do in their childhood, they can do here.

A clown does not avoid difficulties, he magnifies them. He even shows them in a grotesque way to others. Expressing them creates room to lift emotional barricades. In sharing them with others, he avoids the loneliness of having to deal with it all by himself. Clowning heals your inner child; the attention you needed in your childhood will still be given to you by your audience. Even better: a clown receives applause for things that were disapproved of when he was a child!
My own childhood experiences have filled a treasure chest with heart-aches, which I dare to show freely as a clown. For instance:

+ suppressing emotions — playing freely
+ having received a lot of criticism — my clown is able to bear things very well
+ being told to be modest — as a clown I like to receive applause
+ not being fully noticed — you can look at my clown elaborately
+ receiving conditional love — my clown's love is unconditional

## ↦ Freedom ↤

*"A clown symbolises the human desire for freedom. Freedom to be yourself entirely and to surrender with complete confidence to others and to life itself. Like a child does unconsciously. Like an enlightened person does consciously." (1)*

It is good to realise that a clown exists by the grace of the audience and that he is carried by the interaction that exists between them. It is also good to realise that a clown is trustworthy and that he poses no threat. His sincerity encourages people to open up. Frequently performing as a clown and experiencing this freedom makes you freer.

In order to return to the freedom of your inner child, you need to investigate your deepest desires. What do you *really* want in life, without compensating your desires over again for the people around you and their expectations? It requires courage to do what you want to do most and remain loyal to yourself. To go wherever you want to go, even if others do not want you to. You do not intend to disappoint others because of this; you are merely honest and you want to live your life based on free choices.

A friend of mine had been working in the office of a concrete and steel construction company for thirty-five years. When computers were first introduced, he could not keep up with his work. He got ill, had a burnout, and stayed home for a year. In a conversation at a reintegration agency, he was asked what he really wanted to do. He replied, 'I would like to become a clown'. From early childhood he had ached to live this dream, as he had always been so very fond of the circus. He was lucky that the reintegration consultant encouraged him to start following a clowning course. This is how he ended up with me and later on with other teachers. A few years later, he got employed as a Cliniclown (the Dutch term for a clown doctor in hospitals). I think this is a wonderful example of returning to your deepest desires.

*"A clown holds up a mirror and lets you look beyond your limits."* (1)

By holding up a mirror the clown can help you break down false appearances. This will offer you a better perspective on what is possible for you and what isn't. The fact that I keep myself busy with clowning says a lot about my own quest for freedom. I like doing things my way and I like to do things how and when I want, without intending to be selfish. Being an adult, I consider it a challenge to return to my inner child and dare to be guided by my emotions and impulses. This happens automatically when I perform or teach. At those moments, I feel energetic and happy, and energy courses through my body. My clown helps me to process difficult things from my past and to live openheartedly. I become melancholic when I do without clowning for a longer period. Falling back into my ever so familiar dissociative behaviour is something I would like to prevent; I disconnect with others as soon as they appeal to my emotions too much. I have to avoid running away, withdrawing myself or keeping quiet when someone becomes angry. My challenge is to keep in contact and to feel exactly what is happening to me. And to express this.

*"Our inner clown connects us to our human emotions. He leads us to the heart. He has a close connection with the Inner Child and is subjected to all the emotions that Normal People also have. But he keeps communicating and making contact."* (1)

When I can express the love I feel for other people through my clown, I feel happy. Nowadays, my clown does this more actively than he used to. Obviously, you cannot perceive his and my development as two separate things. I used to be more passive and this was reflected by my clown. He was more like an spectator, observing the world from his safe spot on the suitcase. I have become more open and forward in my encounters with other people, and so my clown also shows more initiative. He sits less on his suitcase, and rather walks up to people. More and more does the clown show me what I look like inside, and why I do things the way I do. Moreover he shows me that following my heart sets me in the right direction.

"I believe that, as a child, you are very close to yourself, that you are honest to yourself. During your life, that honesty partly disappears; we need to relate to others in that strange, social web and in that, we deny ourselves. Then, there is a way back; you try to be closer to yourself again." (15)

↔ *Little Clown* ↔

I met a tender and fragile girl
I saw her suddenly, throughout my whole life
she was wearing a little red nose
and a red-checked dress
and her eyes were beaming with love and with pain

once, long ago, she came down to earth
her being filled with but one thing
to be love
to beam and to give unconditionally
a hint of the divine among humanity

no one seemed to notice what she carried with her
nor seem to enjoy how beautiful she was
her form and her love were disapproved of
and forced into a straightjacket of hate

in utter confusion and pain
she decided to quit being love
she, too, came to believe in the lies
'I am sinful, all good comes from above'

for protection a huge 'No' was born
in which all her tenderness had a place
'to live means to suffer and mankind is lost'
no wonder she disappeared from the stage

but a clown opens all doors
as he merely consists of 'Yes'
full of wonder for the glory of life
with a heart that embraces all
so vulnerable that he is indestructible

and so the tenderness was freed from the 'No'
accompanied by a wave of deep, deep heartache
and in the mirror I met my reflection
a very tender and fragile girl
wearing a little red nose
and a red-checked dress
and her eyes were beaming with love and with pain

welcome to my life
my arms, my heart
sad, sweet, little clown
touchingly tender and wonderfully beautiful
wanting nothing but to be love
you are a miracle
a gift from god


*Anna*

# 4. Feeling and intuition

*"If you start living intuitively, it is better to use words as little as possible. Silence makes room for feelings. The mind hinders feelings." (16)*

*i* f you suppress your feelings, you disrupt the vitality in your life. Emotions that cannot be expressed freely will eat you up inside. At times that I did not feel well, I often pushed myself (an echo from my childhood: don't whine, just do it). Even during my courses and performances (other than my non-verbal clowning) I hid my sadness, I worsened my sore throat and I ignored all my insecurities. Unnatural and extremely exhausting.

Fortunately, since recent years I dare to express my doubts more often and share them with others. I have become gentler with myself. I don't always take cold showers anymore after sports because it supposedly makes me tougher, I stopped bench pressing heavy weights to become stronger, nor do I mind a bit of a belly anymore. In essence, it means that I learn to let go of wanting to be in control, and I stopped striving too much for perfection. I dare to show more of the real me, without the fear of not being liked or not doing the right thing. Of course this feels liberating, but it also makes me feel insecure. Am I too vulnerable, too gentle, or too transparent?

*"We do not treat our feelings kindly. We often do not even realise that we have them and can use them for our benefit. People who say: 'My feelings tell me...', are often perceived as weird people, who apparently do not have enough intelligence to say clearly what they mean. Feelings are mistrusted because they cannot be explained through reason. That is why feelings are repressed and we prefer a rational explanation." (16)*

I always thought that I could sense things well. Until I found out that I confused this with being sensitive. Beautiful music, a good film, or a magnificent book could move me to tears. But did I feel that anywhere in my body? I could not say, because my feelings were, apparently, regularly sabotaged by my thoughts. I have often cursed my occupied head, because I have a strong desire to live from my gut instinct, my feelings. And yet I came to realise that my ongoing stream of thoughts is also valuable. It keeps me sharp and enables me to make decisions. What if I could only feel, and based my actions on those feelings? Life would become a sea of emotions; my emotions would engulf others, and in this sea I would drown. Strictly acting on impulse during performances could result in me completely losing myself, and hurting people physically or emotionally. For instance, if I would see a child with a mouth-watering strawberry ice-cream and I would suddenly grab it – after all, clowns simply love ice-creams – then I would have gone too far.

*"In our society, the emotional life is usually resisted. While it is beyond doubt that creative thinking – as well as every creative activity – is inseparably connected to feelings, it has become a goal for us to live and think uninfluenced by emotion. Being 'emotional' has therefore become equal to being unwholesome or unbalanced. However, by accepting this criterion, one is significantly weakened and one's thinking impoverished and numbed." (17)*

For some people it is hard to be silent or to do nothing for a moment. Silence allows for your emotions to surface. This is not always pleasant. Perhaps you know the feeling of tension in your belly when you had to share a lift with strangers for just too long. Nobody says a word and you feel uncomfortable, but you do not say anything.

When you are clowning, it is essential to get in touch with silence.

Moments of peace and quiet give a clown, and his audience as well, time to experience things more intensely and to process various stimuli. From that silence a smile can easily emerge. This smile is often a sudden release of built-up tension. And what goes for the smile, naturally also goes for poignancy, wonder, or any other emotion.

I register many stimuli from the outside world every day. As a clown, this offers many opportunities for play, but for me personally, it is difficult. Because I do not spend enough time feeling impressions, I hardly experience them adequately. But when I do succeed in this, I respond more clearly and openly. Haptonomy, body work, and meditation have taken me a long way, but in the end I tend to feel most when clowning. At such moments my energy flows and I feel more balanced. I also experience my love for others better.

In the following paragraphs I will help you in getting in better touch with your feelings. I will do this through the clown's life philosophy, personal experiences, and playful exercises. Do not be too harsh on yourself if the exercises don't go the way you want them to. Remember that clowns, too, have bad days...

## Exercise 8: I feel...

*Goal:* to become aware of what you feel and how you can change it.

This is an exercise that requires two participants. Try to be completely present with all your attention, in touch with yourself and with the person standing opposite you. Both of you will try to express the feelings you experience. Please note: Feelings can change per second!

1. Stand opposite each other, about 3 or 4 metres apart. You both close your eyes and find peace within you. See whether you can sense any feelings inside your body: tension, warmth, turmoil.
2. After a little while, open your eyes and look at each other, without trying to express anything.
3. Now, in turns, say what you feel. For instance, 'I feel peaceful.' Note that you really express what you feel and not just the cause or the result. If you say, 'I feel stupid,' you do not say what you feel

inside, but if you say 'I feel sad because I act stupid,' you do. If this does not work, express the physical feeling, 'I feel that my breath is shallow, I feel my bowels rumble, my feet are cold.'

4. Take a short pause after the description of each feeling, and then feel again. It is possible that you feel something different three times in a row and your partner does not. That is completely okay. Keep on saying what you feel, even if it changes rapidly, and maintain eye contact with the other.

5. Take your time for this exercise and stop when you or your partner decides you've had enough.

*Reflection:*

✣ Were you able to feel something in your body, and if so, where exactly?

✣ Were you able to feel your own feelings or were you influenced by what your partner said?

✣ Were there factors that interrupted your focus on feeling?

---

↦ *Meditation* ↤

*"The closer you get to your clown, the more everything speaks for itself, the more everything goes automatically. There are no obstructions, inhibitions or fears, concerning contact with yourself and the world around you. You function and communicate from your inner core. Life goes by effortlessly."* (1)

The basis of being a clown is to be present in the here and now without thought, as a departure point for acting. A clown has to be attentive to what he perceives inside and outside of him. This way, he becomes part of the ongoing processes of registering (receiving) and transmitting (giving). A clown has an inner void; there is no cupboard full of impressions and memories. Everything is possible and his senses are open; this is how he examines the world.

To me, clowning is trying your very least.

For that reason it can support your clowning to meditate on a regular basis; to find silence and experience its energy. Meditation is directing your attention inward, and this can be done in many different ways. You can close your eyes and sit on a cushion in silence, you can lie down and listen to singing bowls, or you can stare into the flame of a candle for a while. It can be strange to admit silence into your being, but it will bring you closer to your feelings and therefore to your clown.

By meditating prior to a performance, you will get into a deeper concentration and expand your alertness. You will be more able to register what is going on inside and outside yourself and your body becomes open and alert. The more your senses are sharpened, the more stimuli your clown can take in and subsequently transmit. When thoughts are manifested, you will lose contact with the world around you. Being present with your entire body and soul only works if there are no thoughts. Breathing really deep into your belly for a short while will already help a lot. Even then, thoughts will keep on presenting themselves. You can simply acknowledge your thoughts without wanting to use them. Try to say 'yes' to the fact that they are here, without judging them. Next, see if you are able to let them go. The same goes for physical discomforts: an uneasy feeling in your stomach, a throbbing headache, or an annoying itch on your leg? It is there. Observe it and briefly direct your attention to it before letting go again.

Meditation is not only about stopping your thinking process. By letting the busy outside world be, you can experience a unification, a feeling that you are bigger than just your body. At moments like these, the ego disappears into the background, and you just 'are'.

You get closer to yourself and, because of that, you can let go of the need to judge others.

↔ *The senses* ↤

*"A clown has a warm heart, a sensitive body, and his senses are open to the world. He follows a continuous stream of impulses that present themselves, from within and from without." (1)*

A clown is an unusually sensitive and attentive being. Step by step, he registers what happens around him and absorbs all impressions like a sponge.

He:

- ✢ *feels* it when someone gently taps his shoulder. He shows the audience that he has noticed this and responds;
- ✢ *hears* it when someone whispers behind his back that this stupid clown is a big loser, and he will show the person that he has heard him;
- ✢ *sees* that a leaf falls out of the bouquet that a lady is holding in her hands, and he shall comfort the leaf, try to stick it on again, or at least return it to the lady;
- ✢ *smells* the scent of chips coming from the audience and notices that he is hungry as well. He shows the audience that he smells something, follows his nose and lightly licks his lips…;
- ✢ *tastes*, like a child, all kinds of objects that don't look particularly appetising, often to the disgust of any bystanders.

Because of his sensitivity, a clown can perceive attentively what is going on around him. When somebody sniffs, he is already on his way to hand out a handkerchief (contact!). When he sees someone with a photo camera hanging from his neck, he is already posing (contact!). When he sees someone's shoelace is untied, he walks over in order to (clumsily of course) tie it for him (contact!). This way he provides himself with countless opportunities for play.

Apart from being sensitive, a clown needs to be alert. He is always ready to jump to his feet when something happens around him. His outward focus is supported by a fundament of centeredness and presence. Just like a child can lose itself in a game, so can a clown. But by noticing every change meticulously, he keeps his attention focused on each moment. This gives rise to his reactions and any further play, neither being premeditated or prepared.

If, during my courses, a clown enters the stage and carelessly opens (and maybe also closes) a door, then he is obviously not completely in the moment. He skips what is already there because he is too occupied with what he wants to do next. Perhaps he had already worked out an idea or even planned out a whole show.... In that case it is better to start over. I invite him to walk to the door and feel the door handle in his hand. Is it big or small? Warm or cold? Does the door close loudly or quietly? What sounds do you hear around you? All these details can be a starting point for further play. When he senses this, he will experience that each perception is a present, waiting for him. He can immediately start playing with a squeaking door or a door that will not close properly. Before he knows it, a new scene of five or ten captivating minutes develops, especially if he succeeds in including his audience's responses. What he initially planned to show, could perhaps be shown later, or maybe is not necessary to show at all. The power of improvisation is bigger than the possible beauty of a thought up scene. The moment has priority over the plan. Unexpected visitors are usually more fun than scheduled appointments (of course depending on the kind of company...).

All the opportunities for play are already there. You just have to see them.

## Exercise 9: Sharpen your senses

*Goal:* to become more aware of your sensory perceptions, which will refine and sensualise your clowning performance.

You can train yourself, in daily life, to perceive better with your senses. Just take your time for everyday activities and do them more attentively. I will give some exercises. It can be fun to do them with another person, so you can share experiences.

+ *Feel:* When someone shakes your hand, feel if the handshake is strong or weak. Feel if the hand is cold or warm. Soft or hard. Smooth or rough. Dry or sweaty.
+ *Hear:* Sit, inside or outside, on a chair or on the ground and listen to the sounds that are there. Vary your range of sounds, from nearby to further away.
+ *See:* Take a random object and investigate it thoroughly. Take in every detail and make up images or stories to go with it.
+ *Smell:* Don't devour your dinner immediately, but take a moment to take in the scents of all the different ingredients. Also smell at the table, the plate itself, the cutlery, and so on.
+ *Taste:* Eat a plain piece of bread, or with a little butter on it, and take your time to chew. Do not mix all sorts of food or immerse them with extra flavours.

*Reflection:* What (subtle) changes do you experience when you take your time for daily activities?

---

For me, running helps to clear my busy head. My attention is naturally directed to that which is going on inside of my body. I:

... *feel* how the weight of my foot shifts from my heel to my toes...
... *feel* how my feet land and I *hear* the sound of every step...

... *feel* small aches and pains in the joints of my legs and in my stomach...

... *hear* my quick breathing and I *feel* how the air travels through my throat...

... *feel* how sweat drips from my forehead and...

... *smell* and *taste* it too, sometimes ...

... *feel* the wind blowing alongside my head and I *hear* its sound in my ears...

... *taste* the flavour of a chewing gum in my mouth and I *hear* the sounds of chewing...

It feels nice and relaxed when my head has been emptied of thoughts. Soon enough, all kinds of new thoughts emerge. Not so much daily thoughts; there is now space for new thoughts.

Being in the moment means that you do not look back to the past, which is ballast or look toward the future, which is unpredictable. Some people look forward to the summer holidays all year long. Three weeks of doing nothing but lying in the sun! However, when the holidays arrive they don't manage to relax, and thoughts arise about the period after the vacation, about work that awaits ...

You can only feel what you perceive in the moment. You can never feel the way you did when something is over. A pinch in the arm hurts right now, a good pizza is tasty right now and what wouldn't you give to feel that soft kiss again! Nor are you able to feel now what you will experience next week when you will visit that football game. There is only the present moment in which you can enjoy and it is the challenge to do so with all your senses. A statement by Fritz Perls, founding father of the Gestalt Therapy, goes as follows: 'Lose your mind and come to your senses!'

*Goal:* to experience what happens when you are completely in the here and now.

In this exercise, dare to experience 'the emptiness'. Do this exercise with your senses open, without thinking about what you could or should come up with. Calmly and attentively follow the course of things. Take your time. Sometimes it requires some patience and the pitfall is that you might want to break the silence too quickly.

1. Make your clown's entrance in front of an audience with only a teabag in your hand. You have a neutral expression on your face, that says something like: there's not much to expect from me today.
2. Look at the teabag and the audience intermittently. Do not act, but perceive what changes there are in the movement of the teabag and in the responses of the audience. Show when a change affects you, but keep it minimal.
3. Keep breathing to your belly to help you relax, stay patient, and attentively observe what is happening. Perhaps the teabag sways lightly from left to right, swirls around, or bobs up and down like a yoyo. And maybe your arm becomes heavy or a loud laugh comes from the audience.
4. Gradually play more freely with your discoveries. Maybe the teabag can make a double loop or you make the yoyo movements a bit larger (as though you are dipping your teabag into water). As long as it is originated from what is already present and not what you have thought up earlier.
5. You can stop whenever you feel your are finished, but do not stop too quickly.

*Reflection:*
+ What happened inside of you?
+ Were you able to stay calm?
+ Were you able to keep your attention to what you were doing?
+ Did you succeed in sharing your feelings with the audience?

*Note:* You can do this exercise with any object. For instance a towel, a sandwich, a banana, a brush, a piece of paper, and so on.

---

*Goal:* to trust you can create something out of nothing.

You are about to show the so-called 'greatest trick in the world' to someone. This 'marvellous' trick does not really need to have a lot of content. However, it is presented with quite some pomp and circumstance. It comes into existence out of nothing and is created without any attributes; you merely use the support of your body.

1. Wear your red nose. Have someone stand opposite of you and try to empty your head. You know you will have to come up with a trick in a minute, but you have no idea what it is going to be. Whenever you notice only the smallest idea of what it might be, press your inner 'delete button' and start over.

2. Put your body in motion by swinging your arms, moving your fingers, twisting your torso, and so on. Now, find out if these movements may lead you to an idea for your trick. Perhaps your hips sway in an interesting manner, and you direct your attention to this. Or one of your fingers seems to move independent of your willpower. You may see a loose thread on your jumper that dangles exuberantly. These things can function as good starting points, but let go of the feeling that you already need to know where the trick is heading.

3. Once you have started you will continue to develop the upcoming trick step by step. Every change is a step forward. Be patient, as after several changes an idea of where this is leading, will pop up. Always stay in contact with what is happening in the moment and do not forget to enthusiastically share your developments with the other person. When it turns out to be an uphill struggle, keep on believing that something will come up eventually.

4. At a certain point, the greatest trick in the world will present itself (note: if nothing happens, simply try again). This can be something really small; for instance, your left index finger may invite your right index finger for an unusual dance, or if you pinch your arm, one of your legs lifts into the air. Obviously, the clown will present this as something sensational!

*Reflection:*
+ Did you notice whether you could guide your body through the entire process?
+ Did you manage to remain calm and develop your trick step by step?
+ Were you able to stay connected to your audience?
+ When nothing happened, were you able to find out what was holding you back at that moment?
+ When a 'great' trick did happen, were you able to feel the excitement of having made it up from scratch?

## 4.1 Make real contact

*"A clown is uncomplicated, open, and pure. He is a yes-man and does not avoid challenges. His life constantly takes place in the here and now and from that basis he makes unprejudiced contact with people around him. In order to be able to do that, you first need to be able to make contact with yourself and your feelings."* (1)

To me, the true essence of clowning lies in the intention to make loving contact with other people. He does this from an unconscious desire, not from a rational consideration. A clown continuously takes steps towards new contacts. A step full of devotion, in all openness, and without any additional thoughts; solely from that unstoppable urge to want to meet and play with other people.

When can you speak of real contact and what does it require?

In my opinion, we could show a more sincere interest in our fellow human beings. We could, for instance, listen to others without directly giving well-intended advice, and simply ask about any contexts or motives. We could also try to see from their perspective, separate from our own ideas and convictions. By respecting deviating opinions, people can come closer together.
Ultimately, looking at ourselves from a different angle creates more space in meeting others. It is refreshing when you do not take yourself too seriously and when you can laugh about your shortcomings.

The fear of making contact can sometimes outweigh the desire to do this. Fear of being too vulnerable and consequently being rejected. Every new rejection can create more pain and further withdrawal. As a result there is silence, no action is taken, and security is sought behind dark sunglasses, cool caps, or tinted car windows. A wall is drawn up for protection; an attempt to shut out the pain. This way the connection with feelings is broken and the pain gets bottled up (think, for instance, of the lead character in Pink Floyd's The Wall). After that, it becomes harder and harder to open up.

Fear is the opposite of love.

When someone is afraid to open up and keeps his feelings hidden, he cannot get involved in an intimate relationship. There is always something in the way. Personally, I am often afraid to say the wrong thing. I hear myself talking very consciously and at the same time I think: 'Did I use the right words? Is this interesting enough? Am I interesting enough?'

My inner critic is present with all the things that I do: 'I hope I am doing it right.' And when I am doing nothing: 'Does someone expect something of me?' There is a hidden fear of rejection, and when the rejection comes, I feel as though I am rejected as a person. The fear of judgement hinders me from living from my core. A child knows no fear while he lives with an open heart. He lives in freedom and likes himself for who he is.

A clown, like a child, has an open mind towards people and situations. He plays from the heart, which links his belly and his head. Emotions are in our belly; it is the place where you feel. Your head, on the other hand, judges, evaluates and looks ahead. Here resides thought. Your heart is in between, directing your actions based on your feelings. It tells you how you feel about things and what to do.

*"Clowns are pre-eminently creatures that thrive on their heart's energy. The true clown plays and pours from his heart, he is heartily present. This is inevitably melting love-energy that captures the hearts of all. In the old days, fools already knew how to 'disarm' their lords and keep them with both feet on the ground. The same way, with loving humour, jokes and amazement, clowns in our time take the opportunity to establish a connection between heart and head, feeling and mind." (1)*

| happy!!! | **angry** |
|---|---|
| s.a.d. | *scared* |

Just like you can become more aware of your sensory perceptions, you can also become more aware of your emotions. Emotions are exceptionally suitable material for clowning. The four basic emotions that drive human beings are happiness, anger, fear and sadness.

All our emotional reactions are based on experiences from our past; they have been conditioned. Perhaps in your childhood, like me, you did not learn to express your emotions fully. When you hide your emotions, they remain bottled up and continue to exist as emotional blockades. Or there is a danger that they erupt in later life. From personal experience I know how hard it is to break free from them. For a long time I believed that my sore throat was strictly a physical condition or the result of misusing my voice, the absence of bass register, or several allergies. Only later did I discover that it was indeed psychosomatic, and that the cause went back all the way to my childhood. At moments of tension or when I was at the centre of attention, I felt my throat closing up and I noticed myself squeaking. The throat is the area that connects to the expression of your emotions. It feels like a cork in a bottle when these emotions cannot be released.

The emotion 'anger' usually has a very negative connotation. If you look beyond, you may discover that beneath anger hides grief. This grief originates from an essentially positive feeling: the desire to achieve something. The moment this desire is not fulfilled, you feel frustrated. This develops into anger and, for some people, it manifests itself into aggressive behaviour. The more grief is bottled up, the more important it is to release that emotion completely. This is easier for children than for adults. When emotions are shown to the outside world, space can be made inside of you.

A clown openly shows his basic reactions and is always in touch with others. He reacts automatically from his subconscious and he does not know the workings of cause and effect. He never wonders what the consequences of an emotional reaction will be. He plays the whole palette of emotion and can instantly switch from one to another. Like a child that falls and cries, he can laugh again two seconds later when he is given a sweet. The new moment replaces the old one. The sweet is the here and now.

*"In a society where emotions are suppressed, clowns magnify all human emotions, thoughts and manners. Everyone can recognise his or her own incapacities and insecurities in a clown. Often a clown looks like a child, although sized like a grownup. Like children he is able to let go of certain emotions. Grief and happiness, laughter and tears, one emotion can change into another in no time at all." (1)*

Observing the behaviour of a child can teach adults how to react in a more direct manner. When a child wants attention (for instance when he is in pain, excited or scared), he demands it immediately. Whether his parents are involved in a conversation, working, or relaxing on the sofa, he simply exclaims: 'Mummy, daddy, look at me!' A child cannot postpone his emotions like adults have been taught. We cannot blame a child for not asking if this is a convenient moment. A child has not developed enough to be able to emphasise with others. First there is an emotion, after that (possibly) thinking, and then reflection. The same goes for a clown, who sometimes looks a little stupid because he is slow on the uptake. He reacts slower than the average person. But the connection with his emotions is usually quite established.

*"When you meet someone who has been hit by an arrow, you do not waste time asking where the arrow came from or what the social background of the archer might be; you do not think about the type of wood of the shaft or how the arrowhead has been made. Instead you concentrate on the immediate removal of the arrow." (18)*

The above is not a plea for behaviour purely based on emotions. It is an invitation to speak more directly from what is going on within you. For example, one morning I went to the bakery for some bread and the bakery girl shuffled toward the counter resentfully. My first thought was: 'What a shame when you have to work all day like that'. So I said: 'I can see from your shuffling that you don't feel like it today'. Perhaps it did not sound very positive, but my intentions were good. However, her reaction was the worst I think you could possibly get. She ignored my remark completely and coolly asked: 'How may I help you?' For a moment I was flabbergasted and felt it in my stomach. I thought it better not to leave it at that, or I might go home feeling bad. So I asked her: 'Did you mind me saying that?' She responded with a smile that this was not the case. To me this was enough. Because I was in touch with my emotions, I could be honest and share my doubts with her. I felt relieved.

↦ *Gibberish* ↤

Since a clown is not an intellectual being, but rather an emotional being, words and thoughts rise up from his belly, impressionistically. Often he says or mutters some words and occasionally some of the words actually exist. He speaks an imaginary language called 'gibberish' or 'jabber talk'. You cannot understand much of it, but the intonation, specific words, and accompanying gestures help give an impression of the essence of the story. Gibberish is especially suitable for expressing your clown's emotions, especially when it somehow doesn't work the normal way. It is also safer because people hardly understand what your clown is saying. He expresses his emotions without addressing someone directly. As a verbal clown it is important to develop a kind of gibberish that suits you, that requires no brainpower but comes straight from the belly.

Some possible forms of gibberish follow below, which you can use as a basis; you will need to season them with your own flavours.

1. A FOREIGN LANGUAGE: for example, Swedish, Russian, Japanese, Hebrew, or any another language you do not or hardly speak (or one you speak fluently, so you can play with it). Choose a few typical sounds and let some specific words recur occasionally, for instance, words from your own language. This gives a funny effect. Do not aim for perfection, but believe in what you are saying and make sure your body is full of energy.
   Example: *'Hur omfattar kraftigt trollstaven snuret on Sunday. Och hur genast handerna fatta spetsen hende tack curtains?'* (this is a Swedish nonsense sentence interwoven with some English words).

2. A DIALECT: you can take a dialect as a starting point and change it by skipping certain vowels or prolonging others.
   Example: *'Bin bezee mikin caows eh pasfoo daes.'* (Been busy milking cows the past few days).

3. ALTERING OF THE VOWELS: replace all vowels with one specific vowel or sound.
   Example: *'Yesterday I went fishing with my grandmother and grandfather.'*
   When all vowels are replaced with an *e*, this becomes:
   *'Yesterde E went fesheng weth me grendmether end grendfether.'*

You can vary with other vowels:

*o:* 'Yostordo O wont foshong woth mo grondmothor ond grondfothor.'
*i:* 'Yistirdi I wint fishing with mi grindmithir ind grindfithir.'
*ai:* 'Yaistairdai Ai waint faishaing waith mai graindmaithair aind graindfaithair.'
*ou:* 'Youstourdou Ou wount foushoung wouth mou groundmouthour ound ground-fouthour.'

4. AN IMAGINARY LANGUAGE: just start making a few sounds, combining them into imaginary words. Keep on talking and see which imaginary language you end up with.

5. ONLY SOME FOREIGN WORDS OR EXPRESSIONS: *Finito! Basta! Vraiment? Quoi? Leider! Skol!* The Swiss clown Grock used to constantly repeat, *'Nicht Möglich!'* ('Not possible!')

6. LITTLE FILLERS OR SOUNDS: *Oooooh! My my! Tsk tsk tsk! Ohlala! Yesssssssss!*

---

## Exercise 12: Little Red Riding Hood

*Goal:* to practice gibberish by altering the vowels.

1. Choose a fairy tale such as *Little Red Riding Hood, Cinderella* or *Snow White.*
2. Read the text aloud, preferably to someone else. While reading, substitute all vowels with other vowels.
3. It is important to use your body and facial expressions to support what you are saying, for example by making a kind of newscast for the hearing impaired. This way the audience will get a better understanding of what you are trying to tell.
4. Speak faster. This will probably lead to more 'mistakes', but the audience will enjoy it more.

*Reflection:*
+ Did you allow yourself to make mistakes or did you try to do it perfectly?
+ Did you manage to use different intonations, which works well with fairy tales?
+ Did a particular type of gibberish suit you well?
+ Did you feel the support of your body language and facial expressions?

*Note:* Of course you can practise with all kinds of texts: poems, lyrics, instruction manuals, and so on.

---

## Exercise 13: Happy and angry

*Goal:* to express your emotions more easily.

In this exercise you will try to express your emotions using gibberish. This assignment should be done in pairs. See if you can vary your timbre, intonation and emotion.

1. Face each other and put on clown's noses.
2. Clown 1 is happy and invites clown 2, in gibberish, to come play outside.
3. Clown 2 is angry and makes clear, in gibberish, that he really doesn't feel like it: he is pottering about and does not want to be disturbed. A happy-angry conversation follows.
4. After a while either of you claps his hands, as a signal that you have to switch emotions. Clown 1 becomes angry and clown 2 becomes happy.
5. Switch emotions a few times and, while playing, try to notice how it feels when your emotions change to the opposite.

Try this with frightened and sad as well. You can also make up new combinations like angry-frightened, happy-sad, and so on.

*Reflection:*
+ Were you able to express your emotions freely?
+ If so, how did that feel? If not, what was the obstacle?
+ Which emotion was easiest for you?
+ Did you manage to switch between emotions quickly? — Was that enjoyable or difficult?

*Note:* Check if the other person did not feel attacked by you.

---

↔ *Spontaneity and intuition* ↔

*"I believe a loving human being should return to being spontaneous. We have to touch and hold others, to laugh with each other, to think of and care about one another. When we do not feel well, we go to a doctor. But the most important needs we hold within ourselves: the need to be seen, to be known and to be acknowledged." (19)*

Grownups lose most of their childlike spontaneity in the course of their adult lives. However, it never disappears completely. How far away it sometimes may seem to be, it is still stored somewhere in the body, and occasionally it comes out. At a carnival celebration, a drinking bout, or a sports match, a mask is sometimes taken off and a playful child comes out. I find it fascinating to see the processes that take place during a football match. The taboo on showing emotions spontaneously disappears, which especially men suffer from in ordinary life. Sometimes there is an ecstatic happiness: men hug each other, cry out, make funny little dances, and occasionally they even kiss each other. When you witness this, you see both the exuberance of a rapturous child and an immense feeling of liberation. There must be a strong desire deep inside of them, there certainly must be.

Our intuition is inextricably connected to our feelings. Many people see it as something rather vague and unreliable, but personally I experience the power of following my intuition more and more. In a performance I often pick out the right people, and in my courses I make suggestions or choose music that are just right in a certain act. I do not believe these are mere coincidences. To me, intuition is composed of an acute ability to feel, being well-balanced, and being alert. You trust that what you feel is based on something. Your senses need to be awake in order to perceive well and act accordingly.

*"All this intuitive knowledge, which is strongest when we are born and weakens as we learn to think instead of feel, this instinctive knowledge is not lost. It has been buried beneath an avalanche of arguments and reasoning that we nowadays need to make the world understandable to us." (20)*

The more your mind takes over, the more your intuition is repressed. This development becomes clearly apparent in Theatresports, a form of improvisational theatre, which was developed by a Canadian named Keith Johnstone. In Theatresports, two teams challenge each other in a series of playful exercises, in front of an audience. At first these were mainly non-verbal, leading to slapstick-like sketches. But over the years, more and more players started making use of language. By illustrating or even explaining the acts with words, ambiguous situations are avoided and potential conflicts do not get the opportunity to develop. Because too much gets explained, the dramatic intrigue becomes less interesting. It also diminishes the risk that things go wrong, when that is just where the fun lies! Words take away a lot from emotions, emotions that the audience wants to experience for themselves. This is also the case in daily life: using ten sentences and twenty adjectives to describe that you are in pain, has less impact than a brief look of pain on your face. Nevertheless I consider Theatresports a delightful form of improvisation, where spontaneous behaviour is stimulated and appreciated.

Occasionally, I give my students exercises they can do in their daily lives. One of the exercises goes as follows: Suppose you find yourself in a situation in which you would like to act on impulse, but you don't because of several considerations. Now you just do so anyway. Do not let your ratio overcome your subconscious.

One of my course participants had a good example. She told me that she had recently posted an important letter, but was unsure whether she had put a stamp on it or not. She then got the impulsive idea to write a letter to the postman and stick it onto the postbox. In the letter was an explanation of her problem, as well as a description of the letter in question and of course an extra stamp. On the envelope she wrote: 'To the postman who will empty the mail box tonight'. She personally thought it was kind of a strange deed and the friends to whom she later told this story thought so too. But the next day she found an envelope in her letterbox, containing the following message:

*Dear sir/madam,*

*When I was emptying the postboxes today, I discovered your note on one of them. In my eight-year career I have never experienced anything like this. In times where a lot of 'our' postboxes are destroyed by vandalism, it is lovely to come across something different.*

*Yours sincerely,*
*Your postman*

*Enclosed, please find your stamp, because the letter already had one.*

A clown will teach you to rely on your emotions. Your emotions will not often deceive you, even though your mind wants to overrule them constantly. Following your emotions and intuition is scary, since you give away control (which often is only a false sense of security). However, doing this will bring you closer to what is going on. No more misleading of the brain, but rather enjoying what your heart tells you; you will find passageways instead of thresholds, let-go instead of need-to-have.

*"A clown is the child within ourselves. The carefree child that dares to show himself unreservedly, feels at ease to be himself and safe in the world around him."* (1)

This chapter concludes with some exercises which will help you learn how to react more intuitively. This will definitely benefit your clowning skills.

## Exercise 14: Please do ask

*Goal:* to give in to your desires.

Being truly free means that you dare to stand up for your desires. That you, like a child, ask for what you need. Think about what it is like for you to ask someone a personal favour. Continue keeping a person in mind, someone who is emotionally close to you, like a partner or a good friend. Would you dare to ask him or her questions such as:

'Could you run an errand for me?'
'Could you give me a warm hug?'
'Could you cook for me?'
'Would you please massage my back for a while?'

When the answer is 'yes', try to accept it completely instead of worrying whether the other person is truly okay with it. Also see what 'no' does to you and if you are okay with it. Don't let it keep you from asking it again another time.

In the coming weeks, really try to ask such questions more often when they come up. Ask your friend to tell you honestly how this was for him or her. And share how you felt to ask such a thing.

Write everything down, including the situations in which you would have liked to show a bit more of your vulnerable side.

*Reflection:*
+ How did you feel asking these favours?
+ When was it appreciated and when did you feel you were being 'reprimanded' for it?
+ To which people was it easier or more difficult to ask these questions?
+ What did this vulnerability bring you (could also be negative)?

---

## Exercise 15: Following your gut feeling

*Goal:* to improve your spontaneity.

Today, try to follow your impulses, instead of ignoring them. Do you want to tell someone you like him or her: say it! Do you want to give someone a compliment on what he or she has achieved: do it! Do you want to give someone a present for no good reason: act on your impulses! This might take some courage, but it will give you some extraordinary experiences. Dare to ignore looks of pity and comments of disapproval. You must realise that it can also be new and strange to others, and that may keep them from instantly responding with enthusiasm. But, secretly, you may just be a source of inspiration to them...

Try to feel acutely what the other person's response does to you, and also ask them what they experienced. Try to share your feelings and write them down, even when sharing them was difficult: how did it make you feel? The art is to not give up too quickly when you have some negative experiences or reactions, and to leave them where they came from: the other person. For example, you impulsively say 'hello' to someone in the streets or you tell a colleague that you are happy that he or she is your colleague, but you get no response. You do not know why, but perhaps the other person is in a bad mood, in deep thought, or surprised.

People who criticise others may very well do this out of insecurity or projection. It is important to remain true to yourself under all circumstances and to continue acting on impulse, simply because it makes you feel good.

*Reflection:*
+ How did you feel when you got a positive or negative response?
+ Were you able to feel it somewhere in your body?
+ When did you feel you held back?
+ Are you able to take it kindly, without judging your own behaviour?

*Note:* Perhaps it gives you more (liberating) energy and less (suppressing) stress. See if you can do this more often in future and make it part of your daily routine.

## Exercise 16: Just do it!

*Goal:* to learn to act on impulse without judging your own behaviour.

It is best to do this exercise together with someone else who can act as an observer. Try to exclude your inner critic as much as possible. So do not think: 'Isn't it really stupid what I am doing right now?'

1.  Wear your red nose and walk around in your room, expressing all the impulses you are feeling. So if you feel the need to touch something briefly, do so. Would you like to drum with your hands or shout out loud? Do not hold back! Do you feel an urge to lie down on the ground, to jump, or to run? Go ahead!
2.  Continue doing this, but now tell the observer out loud what you are about to do. For example: 'I am now going to drum on my chest and shout!' or 'I am going to jump on the sofa!' or 'I am going to count the flowers!'

*Reflection:*
+  When did you feel doubt or even disapproval?
+  What held you back?
+  Which moments did you experience as liberating?

*Note:* Try to find out where your boundaries lie.

---

## Exercise 17: My hobby is...

*Goal:* to stay in touch with your inner strength.

1.  For three minutes, talk to someone about your hobby, your best holiday, your favourite food, or something else you love, with

much enthusiasm. You agree that whoever is listening to you will listen attentively, without reacting verbally.

2. Then for approximately three minutes, talk about another subject you are passionate about. But now, the other person non-verbally makes clear that he is not interested; he looks at you only occasionally, frequently turns his head away, and might even sigh or yawn. Please note: this person should avoid overacting; he has to try to make it look natural.

*Reflection:*

+ Did you become insecure or unbalanced because you paid too much attention to the other's responses, or did you manage to stay close to yourself?

+ Was there a warm feeling in your heart region, agitation in your stomach, did your legs turn weak or did you experience any other feelings?

*Note:* It is okay if you did not notice anything happening inside your body. You can become more adept at this through attentively noticing how your body reacts when you are in contact with other people.

---

## Exercise 18: Perpetual motion

*Goal:* to try to get into a flow.

When my performances do not go as well as I want them to, I usually get up and wake up my body by walking around or jumping up and down. I can waste my time pondering what might have caused it, but my mind cannot solve it. It is my body that gets me back on track again. In this exercise I would like you to experience how something can originate from nothing. You can do this by attentively noticing what your body has to tell you. Do this exercise in front of an audience and show them everything that you experience.

1.  Start with a few minutes of unusual stretching exercises (without nose). Try to reach your limits, and each moment find out what it is what you are feeling. For example, discover how far your left arm can go backwards. And what does it feel like when you are on the floor with your legs up in the air, trying to crawl, or roll over? Move slowly, but stay curious about what your body can and cannot do. Everything is allowed, but let go of the routine of repeating with right the things you already did with left. This is unnecessary; it is important that it is completely unplanned. When you feel the urge to make a sound, because you are struggling or because it hurts a little, do not repress that sound, but let it out freely.

2.  Now put on your red nose and start moving parts of your body. For example, you could flap your arms, stamp your feet, roll your shoulders back and forth, and so on.

3.  It is important to keep up this movement without wanting to change it. Meanwhile, you stay alert and try to notice if the movement changes a little. For example, your left arm might touch your trousers, or your right leg might make a larger movement than your left one. When this happens, you continue this new movement. If you like it, you can even make it larger.

4.  Continue this new movement for a while, until you notice another small difference. You can rely on the fact that, eventually, there will always be changes, even if you have to wait very long. If you stay alert, you will always discover something new.

5.  Feel the joy of discovering each new movement and share your feelings with the audience. You are a playing and discovering child and they had better know it!

6.  Move even more freely and use the entire space available. It will be wonderful if you get into a flow and make sounds that match

your feelings (for instance: 'Wow!' from amazement or 'Yes!' out of joy). Making those sounds will make you feel even freer.

7. Keep this up for a really long time; until you are completely exhausted and then perhaps even longer. This will switch off your thoughts and make your movements more genuine. Keep enjoying what you are doing, but by all means show the audience your exhaustion, or other feelings that are really there.

*Reflection:*
+ Did you experience joy and a sense of freedom?
+ Did you make sounds or were you silent?
+ Did you manage to let go of possible plans and go with the flow?
+ Which movements were more invented than real?
+ Did the audience notice the difference?

*Note:* This exercise could theoretically continue forever. It is a perfect example of what clowning is all about: acting on impulse, listening to what your body tells you, and sharing your emotions with the audience.

---

On the next page you will find a list of fun things to do. These are not creative exercises, just invitations to stimulate your imagination and give you a stronger sense of freedom. It will give your playfulness a boost. A child's world is the clown's playground. Toon Hermans (famous Dutch entertainer, 1916-2000) once remarked: 'I am still playing in the sandbox, only now more people are watching'.

# ↔ List of fun things to do ↔

Go to the cinema in the middle of the day, organise an open mike night at your home, spontaneously give someone a shoulder massage, happily say 'hello!' to everyone you meet in the street, eat your dinner without cutlery, invite people in your street to have a snowball fight with you, write a letter using a fountain pen, then colour or decorate the envelope, invite the neighbours to come over for high tea, give a present to someone who really needs it, buy yourself a cupcake at the bakery, make a night-time walk through the forest, make eye contact with that attractive saleswoman, tell someone you like him or her, go to a performance you know nothing about, bake a pie with unusual ingredients (e.g. a steak-and-blueberry pie), take pictures of each other wearing funny hats, organise a party for your entire street, make a good-news-only newspaper, make your own postcards, write your own radio play with sounds and record it, wear colourful clothes, cover your toilet walls with fun pictures and meaningful texts, decorate your garden with things you would otherwise throw away, buy flowers for your children, write a poem about nature, watch the flame of a candle in silence for five minutes, collect strange objects and speculate about their potential uses, enjoy the weeds in a garden, read a play out loud together with others, cheerfully hold open doors for everyone, skip through the woods, hand out sweets in the train, spend more time playing children's games.

# 5. Playing with the audience

*"A clown loves his audience; he plays with them and gives himself completely."* (1)

*t*here is a crucial difference between (traditional) theatre and clowning. In plays, there usually is a so-called fourth wall, a virtual division between the stage and the audience. There is no interaction between actors and audience. A clown does not know this fourth wall. He reveals all his feelings, thoughts and doubts. A quiet cough from the audience? Chairs shoving around? Someone laughing loudly? The flash of a camera? A clown's senses are open and he registers everything like a radar. He then responds by showing what these incidents do to him. During my clowning courses I sometimes notice that participants give up on their sketch because their partner did not do what they had expected beforehand. They blame each other, which results in disappointment. At this point, I try to make clear that there are fixed rules in traditional theatre but this is not the case in clowning. Clowning has other basic rules. In clowning, all deviations are welcomed with open arms. They are presents – exciting new incentives to continue on. However, some find it hard to perceive unexpected occurrences as new starting points for their act. They hold on too firmly to the existing plot or routine.

Once, during one of my performances, the following took place. I had just bought new braces for my clown's trousers. While I was playing, the left brace kept coming loose. I was quite annoyed, until I realised that I could also accept this inconvenience and use it as an opportunity for playing. So the next time it happened, I walked to someone in the audience, stood close in front of him or her, and made clear that I was in dire need for help. The struggle to fix the suspender, further complicated by my feigned clumsiness which was a tad naughty, became an act in and of itself. A problem was transformed into an opportunity for play. I found this a miraculous experience. It ensured me that during my improvisations new impulses always arise, which help my clown to keep on playing. As long as I say 'yes' to them.

*"Most adults have learned to think logically, to act effectively, and to adjust to all kinds of rules and customs. Often, you are stuck in this way of life. However, as a clown this is the opposite of what you are supposed to do. You ought to stop using mainstream logic and develop another kind of logic: clown's logic. All for the sake of turning the usual into something special and what's special into something usual."* (1)

Rules provide security and changes provide unrest. However, exploring enriches life, while walking away from situations does not lead to any new insights. One of my favourite precepts, especially in times of trouble, is a quote from Nietzsche who once said, 'What does not kill you makes you stronger'. As a clown you sometimes float in a vacuum; there is a massive black hole made of nothing. To deal with this emptiness and trust that movement will come, is one of the biggest challenges of clowning.

## ↔ *A clown is a tango dancer* ↤

For two years I followed Argentinean tango lessons. To my surprise I discovered that there are parallels between tango and clowning: following impulses, clearly indicating those impulses, being able to let go and improvising. Tango is a passionate dance, a journey of the heart between two souls. In this beautiful dance there are leaders and followers. The leader (usually a man) is expected to be crystal clear in the movements and steps that he prompts. It all happens impulsively. Dance-figures are not planned in advance; they present themselves during the dance. The follower (usually a woman) tries to turn off her thoughts and feel what it is the leader wants. In order to achieve this, she often closes her eyes. After all, the eyes only want to 'keep an eye' on what is happening, which interferes with feeling the dance. If you watch a couple dancing tango you often can't determine who is actually leading or following; they have become a symbiotic entity, which is very beautiful to watch.

Performing as a clown, I invite my audience to dance a metaphorical tango with me. I start out sitting on my suitcase, watching people. It all looks innocent and relaxed, but I am very attentive. Which members of the audience show openness? Attention? Warmth? Whom shall I ask to 'dance' with me? My game invites people to connect: 'Come, close your eyes, open your heart, and let's dance together!' I, the clown, want to radiate trust. All the while I keep looking and feeling if the other person truly welcomes me. We both do not know what is going to happen, but will we take on the adventure?

This introductory phase is often followed by an impasse, which is the most interesting phase. It is a short moment of nothing; there is no script or point of departure. This vacuum will lead towards action, but what kind of action? Who is going to make the first move? What kind of move will that be? What kind of consequences will it have for the other person? Will the clown continue to be the leader or will the roles reverse, and will he be led? Ways of playing this game can be found in an upcoming section titled: *The Triangle of Contact*.

### ↬ *Improvising* ↫

*"Discover a place — deep, or not so deep — within yourself; that place from where you can look at a situation as though you see it for the very first time, time and time again. You do this with the curiosity and the amazement of a child who discovers the world without wondering what others might expect, or what is good and what is bad."* (1)

One day, an experienced clown for children visited me. He had asked me if he could come by to talk about improvising with the audience. In my previous meetings with this person, I had noticed that he talked mostly about himself. This time was no different. It started the moment I asked him how he was doing. He said that it had been an excellent year. He told extensively about his performances and that there were more than in the previous year, and that this previous year had also been an excellent year. He talked like this for at least half an hour, showing no sign of interest whatsoever in his host. Eventually I had had enough of it, and I asked him to shut his eyes and especially his mouth for a moment. When he sat in silence, I asked him to name some objects that he might have seen in the room. Unfortunately, he did not manage to come up with anything but the yellow cup and saucer that he drank his coffee from. Not a thing! And you should know that numerous clown's noses were scattered across the wall, where there used to be holes. So I asked my visitor: 'How will you ever be able to improvise as a clown, if you are mostly concerned with yourself and you don't observe what is present around you?' I think he understood. Now the conversation could begin…

With everything you want to learn in life, whether it is how to sing, play the guitar, or hammer throw, you need to master the basic skills first. If you want to play the piano, you have to get acquainted with the keys first and you have to be curious about the instrument. You will have to work hard acquiring basic skills and reading notes before you can play music on it. And you will have to continuously do your scales before you know the basis upon which you can improvise.

The same goes for driving a car. Only when you know exactly what to focus on when driving, how to switch gears and brake, how to act automatically without having to think too much, only then will you be able to drive smoothly, look around a bit and relax. Learning techniques might seem artificial at first, but it ensures that you have the tools for expanding your playground.

Here follows a good metaphor that illustrates the difference between letting go blindly and letting go while mastering certain basic skills. Imagine that you are holding a small ball tightly in your fist. This image represents frenetically holding on to an existing situation. If you drop the ball, you have let go completely. This may cause chaos and uncertainty. However, by putting the ball on the palm of your hand, you can let go while giving support. Improvisation from knowledge, experience and trust.

In order to be able to discover, it is important to let go of your own securities and fixed patterns. That does not mean that you have to throw away everything you know, but there is more. A clown, like a child, wants to discover how something works, moves, tastes, feels, smells, and sounds. All this information enables him to play with whatever he comes across in his world. The many possibilities stimulate his imagination and create room for jokes.

Actually, I used to have only one short clown's act, the rest was a matter of improvising. I only used this act if I felt nervous because nothing seemed to happen. This 'sausage act' started simply with me eating one cold sausage from a jar. I challenged myself each performance to look closely at all facets of the jar and to come up with at least one new joke for my repertoire. I focussed on the label (depicting cows in a field), on the fluid inside the jar (I replaced the fat with water and drank it), and even on the lid (showing the best-before date). This way, there was always something new, and so the act remained interesting for me, too.

One of my principles in clowning is to make good use of the senses. What do the spectators look like? What kinds of clothes are they wearing? What are they saying? What moods do they radiate? Details or deviations can provide a clown with the necessary inspiration. Perhaps someone is wearing a watch on his right wrist, two rings on one hand, or has coloured laces in his shoes. In making this the centre of attention, a clown encourages other people to react. It is an invitation to dive into the game together. Everything that is discovered this way, can later on become part of an act which is constantly enriched.

A while ago I went to a Toon Hermans performance two evenings in a row. I had seen him a lot on television and he made everything look so easy. As though it was complete improvisation on stage. He had been my inspiration in clowning from a very early age. So I was quite curious to see what was truly improvised on stage and what only appeared to be. During the first performance he was very focussed on the audience and fished for reactions to which he could improvise. This happened on a regular basis which I found extremely well done. However, the second night I discovered that a lot of what he did was exactly the way he had prepared it (perhaps there is no other way in big shows).

For example, when he came on stage the first night, he asked his musicians to stop playing since he had experienced the weirdest thing that afternoon. He wanted to share it before the show. He explained he met a woman in the city centre who exclaimed: 'Mr Hermans, I am so glad to run into you. Fantastic, and that on my birthday!' To which Toon responded: 'Congratulations! What age did you reach?' 'Eighty years, Mr Hermans.' To which he responded that in that case they differed ten years. 'But Mr Hermans, are you ninety years old already?!'

The second night he entered the stage and did exactly the same thing. He stopped the music and told the same story the way he had done the night before. I noticed that I was extremely disappointed, as though I had been cheated. This was not the realness I had hoped for. But at the same time I found it quite clever; he had played the act so spontaneously and real, that it seemed entirely new. And to *this* audience it was new. Providing people with the illusion that they are witnessing something new is quite an art.

Of course, when playing a clown, you give form to a character; it is not really you. You try to merge with the clown for part of the day, but when you get to bed at night, you are not wearing your clown's nose... You know this character through and through and sometimes you can predict his actions. Whether you want it to or not, this is how your brain works. It is an illusion to think that the only thing you will have to do is improvise. You will have to combine improvisation with clowning techniques. You can take emptiness as your starting point for play, but it is important to know how to draw reactions. And if you want to do something that you have already done before, people should not be able to notice that. Either something really new happens or you pretend as though it is new. This does not mean your approach can't be warm-hearted.

↔ *The audience* ↤

When I am acting as a clown I hardly feel any fear. On the contrary, I can't wait to perform and plunge into another unknown adventure. I want to meet as many people as I can and I feel privileged that being a clown enables me to do so. Playing with people in a childlike way gives me energy and makes me feel invulnerable. It seems that as a clown I experience a freedom to do what my heart tells me to do. I feel that I am very involved with everybody and I do not lose my balance when my appearance causes little response or even disapproval. Words that come to my mind are: grounded, natural, and solid.

A clown always keeps contact, and his openness invites for the contact to be mutual. He wants to discover how he can join in and considers the other's needs. This can be giving attention, but perhaps the other person rather wants to be left alone. A clown respects that. So far, despite his stubborn behaviour, he still adapts to general mood of his surroundings.

*"Clowns are sensitive, honest people who love the world. They are highly valuable."* (1)

Of course, a clown doesn't enter a stage totally 'blank'. He is there with a purpose, but he is not dependent on the reaction of the audience; his sense of self is inherent. There is a difference between so-called *magnetic* play and *electric* play.

*Magnetic play: a clown draws attention to himself by playing passively.*

*Electric play:
a clown plays by seeking to connect
with the audience.*

Lidwien

In *magnetic play*, a clown draws attention to himself by being present, without addressing the audience actively. He simply sits or stands, or he is absorbed in his own occupations (for example cleaning, dancing, or eating). He is not yet focussed on the outside, but obviously the person playing the clown knows that people are watching him. When there are reactions to his appearance or activities, he opens up to the audience.

In *electric play*, a clown is focussed on the audience from the beginning. He presents himself in full glory and he wants to make contact immediately. In this way, some clowns can be too confronting for people who are not prepared for his directness.

Acting impulsively is only useful and fun when it is done in connection with the audience. Without a true connection, a clown could become an arrogant soloist and perhaps even an annoying ego tripper who does not know his limits. A clown should always want to have a connection because having to be alone is a punishment to him. Like a child needs his parents to affirm his existence, an audience is of crucial importance to him. Their loving attention nourishes him. To accomplish such a state, it is essential for a clown to build up a bond of trust. That often takes a little time.

My clown often switches between these two ways of playing. Sometimes I sit on my suitcase eating a banana as though I am totally absorbed in it, not at all aware of my surroundings (*magnetic*). However, I know that this is an interesting scene to watch and that I draw attention this way. After a while I may open up and offer the spectators a bite (*electric*).

I have once seen a group of clowns serenading a man. They sang cheerfully and I enjoyed their comical pleasure in playing. However, during their performance, they kept on looking around. It seemed as though their thoughts were already with their next encounter. They hardly had any contact with the person they were serenading. Acting this way, they deprived the man of a feeling of exclusivity, a feeling that they sang especially for him. When they had finished, they did not even give a personal goodbye; they simply walked off.

Experiences like these effect me deeply. In all my 30 years of clowning, I have seen and experienced how much people long for true attention and dedication. People want to be seen and accepted for who they really are, accepted for their uniqueness. There is always an emotional exchange when people meet, no matter how brief their contact lasts. Something changes in both states of mind and as a clown I am always curious what that actually is. By giving someone personal attention, there is a moment of recognition. That feels warm. Especially when a clown's eyes linger on a person who has already passed by. For a few seconds, the clown was there especially for him or her.

But what if the spectators do not react? What if a clown is not able to reach his audience? Of course, he will show his feelings of disappointment or sadness and perhaps he will give it another try. He may not understand it at all, but at some point he will accept the situation. However, he will never stop playing; he has plenty of joy to spread, and so he will try for the attention of other people.

It is good to be aware that a clown can stir up many emotions. He sets inner chords in motion that may cause people to laugh warmly, be touched deeply, or experience resistance. This is why it is so important that a clown closely looks at the reactions of his audience during an encounter. Are the people open, awaiting, or shy? Is there true interest, or are people just being polite when they laugh and applaud? Does something change during combined play? Does the clown leave the people with a positive feeling? Does he dare to face it if something did not go well, without walking away from it? By keeping contact, he knows if he is on the right track. He is not afraid to take plenty of time for that. He keeps watching and feeling with all his attention.

*"A clown mirrors all pitfalls and stumbling blocks that we as human beings encounter on our paths; our fears, expectations and desires, our defence mechanisms, blocks and pains. In the mirror of the clown all these things are magnified, which suddenly makes them comical. In this way, a clown makes heavy aspects of life lighter and more bearable." (1)*

Whenever a clown sensitively mirrors external features or typical behaviour, he automatically offers people an opportunity for self-reflection. It is absolutely necessary that a clown acts in a refined manner, or else he might go too far which could cause his act to stop being funny.

Participants in my courses sometimes ask me how they should react to aggressive behaviour of spectators. Props or belongings had been taken away, their path had been blocked, or children continued to ask for attention in a negative way. In re-enacting such a situation, it often becomes clear that there had been too little eye contact with the aggressors, which kept the aggression from ebbing or even allowed it to become worse. To me this is logical, as the pain of not being seen is known to almost everybody and may cause feelings of frustration and aggression.

It is important not to react too quickly when something happens. As a guideline you can adhere to the 1-2-3 rule: count to three before you start reacting. This is an important rule, for if you react too quickly, you react out of habit patterns and social conditioning. Knowledge that is stored in your body, so to say. A clown does not yet possess the skills of an adult: speed, intelligence, an instant drive for problem solving. Everything first has to land a moment, be felt and processed.

## Exercise 19: the 1-2-3 rule

*Goal:* to practise fixating and not to react too fast.

This exercise will help you to stay in the moment without reacting instantly. You will need to do this exercise in pairs. As a clown, you will mirror your partner's gestures, in many various ways. While the exercise is going on, let him coach you and give you suggestions.

1. Wearing your nose, stand across from your partner. He will show you normal, everyday gestures, such as waving, scratching his head, coughing, patting his hand on his belly, pointing at something, twisting his hips and so on.
2. You will observe it attentively without starting to move. Only after three seconds you will react. Do this in a neutral way, mirroring the gestures exactly. Try this a few times in a row, until it feels just right.

3. Repeat the exercise. You can now mirror to the initial gesture in the following ways, bearing in mind to wait three seconds before reacting:

  ÷ exaggerated (make some sounds!)
  ÷ as small as possible
  ÷ in slow motion
  ÷ at double speed
  ÷ arrogant
  ÷ shy
  ÷ angry (preferably with a funny ending)
  ÷ clumsy
  ÷ in love
  ÷ insecure

*Reflection:* Together with your partner, talk about your ways of reacting. Then, if you like, you reverse the roles, so you can also experience what works best.

*Note:* It can be interesting to play with this a little: what happens if I react after four, five, or six seconds? Or even ten?

---

↦ *Fixating — Bearing — Reacting* ↤

Clowning is based on a fixed pattern that keeps repeating itself. This process I call the *F-B-R mechanism*, which stands for: *Fixating — Bearing — Reacting*. It describes a clown's order of proceedings that he constantly follows during his performances.

To spectators, clowning might seem like something that everybody can do easily: 'Everybody calls me a clown because they think I am funny!' However, good clowning demands a lot of practice and the profession of being a clown is often underestimated. It is a true profession that requires many skills.

In clowning, many elements come together. A clown needs to have attention for:

+ himself (what goes on inside?)
+ his fellow clown(s)
+ reactions from the audience
+ continuously engaging the entire audience
+ his surroundings
+ anything that can be perceived through the senses
+ keeping up the energy of the performance
+ techniques (tableau, repetition, pauses, timing, magnification)
+ anything that could turn out funny or touching

All points above need to be observed almost simultaneously.

The *F-B-R mechanism* goes as follows:

+ *F* stands for *Fixating*. Every time something happens (something falls on the floor, someone coughs, a door opens) the clown puts his body into a tableau (frozen image) for a short moment. This way, he emphasises that something happened that attracted his attention. Every change in an existing situation creates a new situation and the clown briefly dwells on that. After that he slowly comes to life and starts to make movements again.
*Note:* Naturally, he experiences a first feeling when fixating; for example, shock, amazement or anger. After fixating, the clown focuses more deeply on that first feeling (bearing) and the emotion becomes more established.

+ *B* is for *Bearing*. This can be divided into two parts: feeling and sharing.

a) *feeling*: the clown realises what has happened and he begins to consciously feel this for a moment. Which emotion is closest to the surface and announces itself first?

b) *sharing*: he does not keep this feeling to himself but shows the audience what he experiences inside.

The bigger the transition from a reasonably neutral fixation to an expressive feeling, the stronger the theatrical effect. But this effect has to match the basis of the actual feeling that was perceived, otherwise it will not make any sense.

✢ *R* is for *Reacting*. A clown's further actions are an extension of his feelings. What kind of impulse comes forward? A clown will act it out uncensored, and continues to react from his primary feelings. Furthermore, he will stay in contact with the audience and observe their reactions.

In Laurel & Hardy films you can see very well how the above rule applies. If Laurel does something clumsy again, Hardy becomes agitated and pokes him in the eye. Laurel is shocked by this and hardly knows what overcame him. It takes some time before he seems to realise what happened. Then he gets angry and he takes revenge on Hardy by banging him on the head with a frying pan. The beautiful thing is that Hardy sees all actions that precede this moment, but he doesn't do anything to prevent it: he bears it completely. Next, Laurel gives a satisfying nod that says: 'serves you right', to which Hardy sometimes turns to look into the camera, helplessly (note: in comedy films, Oliver Hardy was the first actor to bond with his viewers by looking directly into the camera). Not much later Hardy gets back to action to take revenge on Laurel, and so on.

Here is an *F-B-R* example from my own clowning experience:

*Fixating*: One day I was performing in a small park somewhere in France. I saw a large woman, sitting on a chair. She was chatting to a girl, perhaps her daughter. The woman hadn't seen me yet, and I simply stood in a pose, waiting for the moment that she would see me. When that happened, she instantly stopped talking and she ceased her lively gestures. Just like me, this placed her in a tableau, but for her it was probably due to her surprise.

*Bearing*: Now that she had seen me, I finally started moving. I took a step forward. The woman started booming with laughter. Not normal laughter, no, real roaring. I stopped and bore what it did with me. I continued to look at her in amazement. This time, my surprise was not acted but entirely real, and she just wouldn't stop laughing. But I sensed that I shouldn't get too close, because I could see that she found it a bit scary. Then she stopped laughing and looked at me inquisitively. I was searching for some good middle ground: to stand not too close and not too far away. When I stood at a safe distance, she laughed so hard that her huge body swayed backwards, and the next thing I knew she had fallen off her chair, and she was lying on the ground.

*Reacting*: Naturally, this gave me a fright (a new tableau), but I also knew that I shouldn't rush to help her, because it might startle her. So my considerate reaction was to come somewhat closer and see how she was doing from a distance. Fortunately, everything was fine but her fall had broken the magic. She sat down again, straight-faced as if nothing had happened, and I waved goodbye discreetly. The end of a short, but special meeting.

Next, you will find two exercises for practising the *F-B-R mechanism*.

*Goal:* to learn how to keep paying attention.

You can do this assignment on your own, though a real audience is always preferred over an imaginary one.

1.  Collect a few totally different objects (for example a hammer, a ball of paper, a saucer, or a tangerine) and put these together in a plastic bag.
2.  Wear your red nose, take one of these objects from your bag and drop it to the ground.
3.  *Fixate* your pose while keeping your eyes on the object.
4.  *Bear* what effect the falling down has on you and share your emotions with your (imaginary) audience by looking at them.
5.  How do you *react* to all this? In other words: what is the first thing you do in response?

First, drop the same object several times and observe how it falls differently each time. Maybe this time it makes a slightly different sound, or it rolls further away. It is never exactly the same, so your responses may vary as well.
After repeatedly dropping the same object, you can try dropping other objects in various ways.

*Reflection:*
+  Was it hard or easy it was for you to focus your attention on the different ways an object can fall.
+  Did reality differ from what you had perhaps thought in advance?
+  In what ways were your reactions visible from your movements and expressions?

*Note:* It is not just the object that causes changes. You change as well, every second afresh.

*Fixate*

*Bear*

*React*

## Exercise 21: Catch the ball

*Goal:* to apply the *F-B-R mechanism*.

You could call this a traditional clowning exercise, since you play a role rather than from your inner self. This assignment should be done in pairs. You play a foolish August and the other one the dominant and sophisticated Whiteface. It would be best if there is a live audience.

1. Take a juggling ball, a tangerine, or something else that is round and soft and will not roll away when it hits the ground.
2. Leave about five metres between you, the silly August, and the bossy Whiteface. Your only assignment is to catch the ball that the Whiteface will throw towards you, but you will continually fail to catch it. So you do this deliberately, but you pretend that your clown is simply unable to do so.
3. Prepare yourself for the assignment, for instance, by doing stretching exercises, making jokes to the audience, or asking them if you look alright. This is important, as it may help you to catch the ball! You can also start a dialogue with the Whiteface or mimic him (of course, directed at the audience again).
4. As soon as the ball is thrown, you fail to catch it, because you are too busy with yourself and the audience, and the ball hits the ground. Set yourself into a tableau immediately (*Fixating*). See which emotion is released spontaneously (*Bearing*) In other words: how are you *feeling*? *Share* that feeling with the audience. Also look for a moment at your stooge, the Whiteface. He must be disappointed or angry. What does this do to you?
5. You pick up the ball from the ground and give it to the Whiteface (*Reacting*). Show the audience with which emotion you do this. Fortunately, you are given a second chance!
6. You are really looking forward to your next chance and you show this in an exaggerated way to your (fictitious) audience. Again you

show your preparations to the audience – it becomes a sort of ritual now! And of course you fail to catch the ball once more. Although you follow the same abovementioned pattern, your reaction could be different each time. This depends on how the ball is thrown, how you feel at this moment and how the people react.

7. Do this a third and final time. Now, you are standing very close to each other, but of course things go wrong yet again.

You can switch the order around if you want to. For example, you can magnify your disbelief concerning the failure by looking at the ball a second time. This way, you show your audience that you truly don't understand how the ball could have slipped through your fingers. You can also try to avoid the angry gaze of the provoked Whiteface as long as possible, by first looking at the ball, then at the audience, back at the ball, then at your feet, at your failing hands, at the audience again, very, very briefly at the Whiteface – ouch! –, quickly back at the audience for moral support, back at the ball, and so on.

*Reflection:*
✛ Did you manage to take your time for each action?
✛ Did you get in a flow when repeating it the second and third time?
✛ Did you notice at what moments the audience reacted strongly?
✛ Ask them what they liked particularly.

*Note:* When you understand how the mechanism works, you will learn to play better and better.

## Exercise 22: Fail to guess

*Goal:* to stimulate your imagination and creativity.

This exercise is meant to be done in pairs: you as the clown, and your partner. You wear your red nose and start depicting a hobby, a sport, or an activity. Your partner will almost immediately see what you are doing, but he will fail to guess the right thing on purpose. For example, if you are depicting a running person, your partner can say anything but running. It is important to make this a very physical exercise, so that you will train your body and your imagination.

1. You are the clown that nonverbally tries to make clear what you are doing. For example, you are shopping, playing tennis, or watching a film.
2. While you are acting out something, your partner says out loud what he thinks you are doing. However…he purposefully guesses wrongly! If you pretend to have a tennis racket in your hands, swinging as though about to hit a ball, your partner can say 'cleaning the windows!', 'running!', or 'filling in tax forms!'. What he cannot say is 'playing tennis!'.
   At this moment, you will start applying the *F-B-R mechanism*.
3. First, *Fixate* your amazement about the fact that your partner fails to guess the right thing by putting your body in a tableau (frozen image).
4. Second, *Bear* what happens (*feeling*). Which emotion arises first? Is there disappointment, because the other person failed to guess? Amazement, because you thought you acted it out very clearly? Excitement, because your partner made a close guess? In any case, show your partner very clearly what you are experiencing (*sharing*).
5. Finally, *React* by coming up with something new that has to do with what you were doing before. Keep acting out a new relayed element that needs to be guessed. For example, in the case of

playing tennis: elaborate on the tennis ball, the net, the lines, the umpire, the linesman, the deviating scoring system, the caps against the sun, a sweatband, and so on. After each thing you act out, your partner will deliberately take another wrong guess. As a result of his failure to guess the right things, you are stimulated to use your imagination more and more.

6. After about five minutes, the exercise is finished. You take off your red nose and you tell the other what it was you were acting out. Of course he already knew and he comforts you in his own way.

Next, you can switch roles.

*Reflection:*

+ Did you manage to apply each aspect of the *F-B-R mechanism*?
+ Was there space for new movement and free improvisation?
+ Could you manage letting go of your thoughts and indulge yourself with playful energy?

---

I find it very helpful to take a 'clown's-eye-view' when watching cartoons such as Tom & Jerry. In cartoons, much more is possible than in real life; the imagination knows no boundaries. Actions and emotions are immensely exaggerated and as a viewer, you can often see what is coming from miles ahead. For example, there is a trap set for Tom the cat: a giant bag filled with rocks. Jerry the mouse cuts the bag open and all rocks start rolling in Tom's direction. He freezes at the sight of this (*Fixating*) so that now he is paralysed. Consequently, he lets all the rocks hit him (*Bearing*) and of course one last rock hits him on the head. After he has borne all the rocks, he leaves the room battered (*Reacting*). What makes these cartoons even more enjoyable is the fact that often, for a short moment, the underdog takes a quick, tormented look into the camera, so that the viewer may feel for him even more.

↔ *The Triangle of Contact* ↔

*"A clown is constantly and attentively present in the here and now. This is important since he is a creator, this is his territory, here lie the foundations of his jokes and concoctions." (1)*

A clown's essential goal is to meet other people, even if he decides to start with magnetic play. In this regard you can define a clown as a proactive character. This means that he walks up to people rather than waits for an invitation (reactive). You can compare it with a waiter who, when you are sitting at a table outside a café, comes to you of his own accord, instead of a waiter whose attention you constantly need to draw before you can order anything.

Of course there is constant interaction during clowning. It is never just one or the other. But this is about the basic principle that a clown's direction is forward. When he makes his entrance, a spectator will soon see what he is all about. He radiates something selfsame; he has typical movements and a characteristic way of doing. He shows his unique self without trying. This is who I am! He is completely himself and he does not come to simply 'take'. With which I mean that despite the audience nourishes him, he is not *dependent* on their reactions. They will not alter his being. In fact, he comes to 'give', himself and all that is inside of him: his cheerfulness, his friendliness, his openness.

The interaction between a clown and his audience occurs according to a particular pattern. I will explain this with the help of the *Triangle of Contact*. Where the *F–B–R mechanism* describes the playing technique, the *Triangle of Contact* sheds light on the order of the steps to follow during performances.

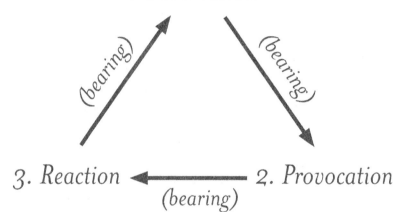

*Observation:* When a clown enters the stage for the first time, he tastes the atmosphere of his surroundings. Sometimes he waits somewhat expectantly. He takes his time attentively observing everything. In fact, he briefly studies the area and the people. What do they look like, what are they saying, and what are they doing? He registers everything that is striking, deviating, and inspiring. During this phase, a clown might appear rather passive, but in reality, he is anything but. He is 'working' really hard.

*Provocation:* In this phase, the clown takes the initiative more and he sets his performance in motion by 'provoking' his audience. I use this term in a positive way: he will undertake something in order to stimulate the audience, thereby inviting them to play along. For instance, he can look at someone in a yearning, endearing, or in a curious way. Like this, he challenges people to react and by doing so he provides himself with 'playing-fuel'. He becomes more active now.

*Reaction:* He registers the audience's response to his actions with great attentiveness. Like a machine, he processes all input and from the multitude of responses, he selects only one or two. This happens in a split second; it is steered by his emotions and intuition. He plunges into the performance. He is now completely in his element.

After completing the triangle, the clown slows down for a moment in order to return to observation. Doing nothing and creating expectant silences every now and then can be beneficial. It makes the audience all the more keen to find out what might happen next. In the meanwhile, the clown keeps looking around attentively and again tastes the atmosphere. How are the people doing this time? Have they loosened up already? Or are they still waiting? Next, he will try to 'provoke' again in order to bring his performance to a higher level, and to loosen up the spectators even more, so that he can, in turn, respond to them.

During the entire performance, he keeps tuning in on his surroundings and checking how his actions come across. This pattern of challenging and responding repeats itself non stop. This is one of the hardest parts of clowning: finding the right balance between sending out impulses and receiving responses that were generated by those impulses.

Because of his open way of communicating, the audience can easily bond with the clown, and a heart connection may ensue. During my performances I notice that I have a natural inclination to establish contact with people based on love. I show them that I appreciate their presence very much. And what you send out, you get back. It is wonderful to see how warm-heartedly people respond; a returned smile, a bold wink, a soft stroke across my head, and sometimes even some money or a present. At such moments I feel happy like the child with a new pair of shoes.

## Exercise 23: Teddy bear talk

*Goal:* to practise the *Triangle of Contact*.

If you don't have an opportunity to practise the *Triangle of Contact* as a clown, you can still try out the underlying ideas by doing the following exercise. You can do this on your own. You are to have a conversation with a teddy bear that you like. If you do not have a teddy bear, buy one that you like a lot. Take your time to choose the right one, the one that moves you the most. During the exercise, try to summon a childhood feeling and based on that, have a complete conversation with your teddy bear, the way small children do.

1. Wear your nose and look at the teddy bear as though it was a living being.

2. *Observation*: look at the teddy bear attentively, and pose a first question based on your perceptions. If you see that its head is slumped, you could ask for instance: 'Hey little bear, are you feeling all right today?'
3. You don't need to let the teddy bear answer as though it was a puppet show, but you can imagine what kind of answers it might give.
4. *Provocation*: then, make a challenging remark: 'What long ears do you have!'
5. *Response*: make your teddy bear flap its ears and then you could say, for example: 'Hey, I can do that too. Look!' To which you make the same movements.
6. Try to find something on your bear that you had not noticed before; a fluff, a hand with only four fingers, or a small change in expression. From this observation you go through the entire process again.

*Reflection:*
+ Were you able to lose yourself in this exercise?
+ Did you manage to keep the 'conversation' going with provocative questions or actions? - Was this silent teddy bear enough of a challenge for you?
+ Perhaps you need other attributes?

---

↔ *Stay in contact with the audience* ↔

A clown automatically establishes a strong bond with his audience; he does not need to make a lot of effort to achieve this. He knows no reasons to hide his emotions. His vulnerability and often his cheerfulness too, call for a dialogue. If you want to communicate openly as a clown, it is important to know your own emotions well: how do I feel about this? Only after you know this, you are able to share your emotions in honesty. But the person behind the clown needs to keep possible personal pain away from the interaction. You speak of personal pain when you cannot distance yourself from your own emotions, and other people's reactions get too close to you. When you are the observer of your own emotions, you are in control. But as soon as these emotions take over, it is no longer a game. Things come too close, they become too real. Remember that responses from the audience are aimed at the clown and not at the person behind the clown. Very often, the boundary between the clown and the person behind him is very thin, considering that a clown's character is based on the actor's personality. Because a clown transforms his actions and emotions, he helps the audience put things into perspective and feel safe making contact. Only when you manage to accept yourself with all your imperfections, you can let the pure clown come out freely.

Making contact with the audience is necessary for allowing the spectators to peek into the clown's inner world. As a teacher, I notice that the continuous sharing of emotions – at exactly the right moment – is one of the hardest parts of clowning. Course participants are often so much focused on their performance partner or on the invention of new ideas, that they simply forget to make contact with the audience. I then tell them that a clown directs 90% of his attention towards the audience and only 10% towards his companion. Maybe that is a little exaggerated, but it indicates the importance I attach to communicating to the audience. A great difficulty in doing this obviously lies in the fact that in normal life it is not polite to focus on other things while you are speaking to somebody. So it is very hard to alter this firm pattern. The timing of looking in the direction of the audience is also very important, because often when the players think about doing it, the right moment has already passed. The desired effect on the audience may not be achieved if the reaction is a split second too late.

## Exercise 24: Feel and share with the audience

*Goal:* to feel and share directly with the audience.

Together with a colleague, you play a scene that is entirely improvised. Playing in front of a real audience is preferred. The goal is to share your experiences and feelings with the audience right away.
Both clowns explain to the audience everything they see, feel and do. I call this technique the 'inner director'. You give an external voice to the voice inside your head that directs your thoughts, feelings and actions. This method offers good support in consciously following your actions step by step. It is important to say *everything* you see, feel and (intend to) do, out loud, *exactly* at the moment that something occurs. Remember that every change, how small it may be, gets a clown's attention.
Let me give you an example.

Clown 1 is situated in a room alone, busy with an everyday routine. This can be anything from watering the plants to eating from a jar of sweets, or even singing. You name it. Right now, he is dancing and suddenly a second clown appears. Things could go as follows:

+ *Clown 1 says, while he keeps dancing, to the audience:* 'Hey, I see a clown!' *Short pause.*
+ *Clown 1 looks at clown 2 and says in the direction of the audience:* 'He is wearing strange clothes.' *Short pause.*
+ *Clown 2 takes a few steps.*
+ *Clown 1 looks at clown 2 again and says to the audience anxiously:* 'Help, he is coming towards me!'
+ *Clown 1 stops dancing and turns his gaze at clown 2 again.*
+ *Clown 2 turns to the audience and says with surprise:* 'Why has he stopped dancing?!' *Short pause during which he looks at Clown 1.*

+ *Clown 2 says to the audience:* 'I am now going towards him.'
  *He then does this.*
+ *Clown 1 nervously to the audience:* 'Help! He is coming closer!'
  *Short pause — he looks expectantly at Clown 2.*
+ *Then he says to the audience:* 'I am scared!'
+ *He takes a few steps backwards and says to the audience:* 'I am taking a few steps backward.'
+ *Clown 2 asks the audience:* 'Why is he walking away?'
+ *He comes closer to Clown 1 and asks him:* 'Do you like my clothes?'

And so on.

There are three versions of this exercise.

## Version A (non-verbal)

1. Before you start, make sure there is a table and place an object on it that has some emotional value to you, for instance a delicious chocolate bar, a pretty necklace, or a ten euro note.

2. You both enter the stage as clowns from behind a door or curtain. Give each other time to make contact with the audience first. Do not focus on the object, yet.

3. Suddenly, you both discover the object. You are surprised, curious, and eager to have it. This way you create a conflict, which makes a good start for a scene. Improvise a non-verbal scene based on the contact you have established with each other and with the audience.

4. Keep directly sharing your emotions and experiences with the audience and do not begrudge each other the attention. I mean that you should give the other clown enough time to perform. *Note:* focus can also shift to the audience if they start to interfere with the performance.

5. Continue playing until you feel that it has been enough. Try to detect when that moment has arrived. One of you can take the

initiative to end the scene. You can do this, for example, by exaggerating your emotions. For instance by crying loudly, weeping, or manipulating, because you don't get the chocolate, the necklace, or the money. After getting what you want or failing in your attempts, you can leave the stage As you leave, both you and your partner show your feelings.

*Reflection:*
+ Was there enough attention for each other?
+ Was the audience involved sufficiently?
+ Was there enough sharing and did this happen at the right moments?
+ Didn't the object receive too much attention?

*Note:* I want to note that a happy ending does not have my personal preference. Like with the endings of many Hollywood films, this kills or neutralises the strength of distinction by contrast.

**Version B (verbal)**

Now you are going to play the scene as described in version A, but this time verbally.

1. Again, put an object on a table, both of you enter as clowns and you start improvising.
2. Both of you explain aloud to the audience everything you see, feel, and (are intending to) do. It is important that all actions, thoughts and feelings are named. Try to be precise and do not skip anything. Take care to turn your face towards the audience and actually look at the people. To me there is a difference between looking in that direction out of obligation (which is merely a technical action) and looking attentively (which is a conscious action).
3. Allow for possible changes as the scene develops.

4. Every time one of you forgets to share his thoughts, feelings or actions with the audience right away, the spectators may shout: 'Audience!'

*Reflection:*
+ Were you able to put your 'inner director' to work?
+ Did you manage to continue sharing with the audience?
+ Did the audience react more when you shared?
+ Did this make the performing harder or easier?
+ What changed about the interaction between the two of you?

## Version C (verbal and non-verbal)

In this third version you play the same sketch, yet again. You start off talking, but after a while you switch to being non-verbal. Be careful not to exaggerate your mimicry. If you 'illustrate' (like sign language for the hearing impaired at a newscast), you suppress the emotions that you wanted to make clear. So it is better not to convey with your index fingers that you are crying, but simply show a sensitive, moving look to the audience. This will have a much stronger emotional effect on the audience.

1. Follow the instructions from version A (possibly with other objects).
2. After a few minutes, switch from verbal to non-verbal.

*Reflection:*
+ Do you think you could convey the same things nonverbally that you did verbally?
+ Was it more, less or different?
+ Did you notice a change in contact with your partner or with the audience?
+ If so, did you experience it as a positive or a negative change?

Doing this exercise may seem a bit artificial, but the more you practise it, the more self-evident it will become to do so. By applying the method of the 'inner director', a clown opens up his emotional life to the spectator directly. At the same time, an immediate connection between the clown and the audience develops. When a clown makes his—sometimes naughty—plans known beforehand, the audience may react spontaneously: 'Don't do that!' or 'Yuck, how disgusting!' or 'Look out, behind you!' Ingredients enough to create a dynamic interaction.

Because of the clown's transparency, the audience sympathises with him and they become attached to him. He can move people like young, playing children can. We may learn from this to, more often, show our emotions openly. When you dare to unrestrainedly show your emotions to the people around you, you invite them to make contact.

Openness creates connection.

↔ *Energy and rest* ↔

*"A real clown comes from within; it's about the faith and perception with which the act is performed." (1)*

Being present is essential to me during a performance. I have found out that if I walk around as a clown without powerful energy, people merely glance at me and continue their way. The border between being present or absent can be very delicate. When I send out a powerful intention to make contact, an energy field will come into existence that stops the audience and makes them watch my performance, enthralled. Even if I am just sitting on my suitcase, looking around....If I do this with all my attention, people will wait curiously for what may be about to come.

Just before a performance, I always imprint the image of a tiger into my mind. He is hungry, and hunting for a juicy prey. The tiger makes me alert and this is reflected by my attitude and my eyes. However, someone once pointed out to me that my look was so intense, that she clammed up and withdrew herself. In being so focussed on the external world, I apparently drifted too far away from myself, and I gave the other insufficient space. Finding a balance between true presence on the one hand and receptivity to external impulses on the other hand, is a real challenge to me.

It is often said about music that the rests and the silences are what actually makes it so powerful. As a person, you become more visible when you radiate rest and tranquillity. Like this you show yourself, without having to make extra efforts.

I once saw a beautiful example of this. I visited an open lesson for a clowning course. Half of the clowns came from Spain, the other half came from the Netherlands. Each clown entered separately and introduced himself in a special way to the audience. The first three clowns were Spaniards and there actions and mimicry were very lively. There was too little room for the audience to process all the impressions and therefore the response was half-hearted. Next, it was Annet's turn, my clowning partner. She had wrapped a thick rope around her body. She entered very calmly, and the only thing she did was give the audience a goofy look and swing the rope a bit. The audience doubled up with laughter. Her individuality had lots of space to reveal itself, and people were given the opportunity to connect with her clown. The power of rest and simplicity.

*Goal:* to experience that peace and quiet can be powerful tools.

Try doing this exercise as long as possible. You will stand in front of an audience without wanting to do something. Simply stand and watch. Before entering, make sure you are very alert. If you feel a lot of tension, focus on the breathing in your stomach, and sigh deeply.

1.  Ask someone to be your audience. Put him or her on a chair and go somewhere the other person cannot see you, for example behind a door.
2.  Wear your red nose and make a calm entrance as a non-verbal clown. Do not act, just enter as yourself and look around attentively.
3.  The first thing you notice, obviously, is that you are not alone. There is an audience and you are allowed to show how you feel about that. Are your surprised, happy, shy, or a bit nervous? Next, look around very quietly. No initiatives should be expected from you today.
4.  You are passive and you register everything that happens around you. Do not make things up; your body or your audience will automatically offer you impulses to play with. Take your time and have faith that there will be movement, sound or reaction. Maybe there is some sudden laughter. This is no coincidence because laughter is often the result of retained tension. The laugh just needed to be released! Give a brief non-verbal reaction through your attitude or expressions. By doing this, you show that you noticed it.
5.  Is there no reaction after all? Then follow an impulse. For instance, if you feel like laughing because you find this exciting, do not hold back! Or do you feel an itch in your legs? Jump up and down!
6.  Next, go back to your basic pose: a neutral look towards the audience. See what happens next.

*Reflection:*

+ What was it like to be in the centre of attention without wanting do to things or thinking that something funny needed to happen — to simply be present and aware?
+ Did you manage to remain calm and continue waiting?
+ Did you experience inner power; a natural, primeval way of being present? If not, keep on trying.

---

To sum things up, playing and mingling with the audience requires a clown to have an amiable disposition and complete awareness of his own body. Moreover, he needs to be energetic, so that he can act quickly and efficiently. If he uses his senses optimally, he will see that there are ample opportunities for interesting twists to a performance. These may be his own impulses or reactions from the audience.

# ↔ 10 tips for clowning in the streets ↔

1. Try to find a friendly way of making contact with the audience. It is often a good start to wave (opening) and squatting or bending down for children (same height). Take your time, so people can see that you are trustworthy.

2. Try to show your uniqueness through your special features and characteristics.

3. Watch carefully how people respond and try to integrate their reactions into your play. Open your senses: What kind of clothes are people wearing? How are they standing? What are they saying? Feel free to challenge people a bit, and tease them kindly (Provocation).

4. Don't be afraid to work with tension and don't go too quickly. Stop in front of people and see what will happen in the silence. Stay attentive. You don't have to know which way the performance will go, just stay focused.

5. Take people seriously and don't make a person look silly. Be open and inviting.

6. Don't make physical contact too quickly. Try to feel when it could be possible to do, but give the audience a chance to make it clear if they do not want this.

7. Try not to be a nuisance to others who have acts or attractions in your vicinity.

8. Regularly make contact with other people that stand nearby. Show them what you are experiencing and see if you can invite them to join you in your performance.

9. Make sure that you are the director and stay the director.

10. Always stay positive! Don't take possible offences personal. People see a clown and don't know you personally. Fortunately clowning amongst people is usually very pleasant and the clown a welcome guest.

# 6. From the heart

↔ *Listen* ↔

When I ask you to listen to me
and you start giving me advice,
you have not done what I asked.

When I ask you to listen to me
and you begin to tell me why
I shouldn't feel that way,
you are trampling on my feelings.

When I ask you to listen to me
and you feel you have to do something
to solve my problem,
you have failed me, strange as that may seem.

Perhaps that's why prayer works
sometimes, for some people,
because God is mute,
and doesn't give advice to try to 'fix' things,
He just listens, and lets you work it out
for yourself.

So please listen, and just hear me
and try to understand me.

And if you want to talk,
wait a minute for your turn,
and I promise you
that I will listen to you.

*From: 'Loving each other' by Leo Buscaglia*

*"Being a clown is not about the nose, it's about the heart." (1)*

*i*f you want to communicate openly and honestly with each other, it is necessary that you try to understand the other. When you firmly hold on to your own convictions, there is little room for another's way of thinking. Showing genuine interest and truly wanting to know what is going on with someone are the ingredients for open communication. In order to really listen to someone's opinion, your ego needs to take a step back. You can only make contact when your heart is open.

I was once invited to observe a group discussion at an organisation which preceded my workshop 'clowning and open communication'. The group had difficulty getting the discussion started and, at some point, someone said that he was fed up with the same people always being quiet. He named which people he was talking about, and a negative vibe was created. I suggested to the speaker that he should address these people directly and ask them why they never spoke. He agreed and in response to his question one man told him that he did not feel comfortable enough in this group to say anything. Someone else said that he almost never had the nerve to say anything, but that he was involved. Another man stated that he preferred listening and that he would definitely speak up when he did not agree; it certainly did not originate from disinterest or a lack of involvement. This came as a surprise to the speaker. He admitted that he had too quickly jumped to conclusions.

*"The more variety we let in our lives, the richer our experiences will be. You are only able to enjoy variety if you are not focused on differences and passing judgements, for example, if you are checking constantly whether you are better than someone else. Doing that means you are comparing and therefore polarising. Whoever handles differences this way will not be able to make contact with the soul of the other. Your heart is closed and you surrender yourself to your ego, which likes comparing and competition. Whoever approaches people with an open heart, does this from his core." (21)*

Clowns are affectionate by nature and have an eye for what is going on around them. This is why more and more they are asked to perform for sick children, mentally disabled people or demented seniors. They seem to strike a chord, and doors are opened that were previously only slightly ajar. Clowns that do this do not burst through the door like overwhelming jokers, but they try to find out, from a gentle beginning, what someone needs (Observation). They are called 'contact clowns', 'modern clowns' or 'gentle clowns'. They show people how much fun it is to laugh together, cry together, or simply not to know what to do together. Their way of working is pure and kind.

*"A clown is someone who is able to make his own tragedy recognisable for others. What most people do not dare to do, he does in public. A clown does what normal people only do in the company of their mothers or partners." (1)*

A clown is at his finest when his vulnerability invites people to join him in his play. When he has an eye for seeing their emotions, it gives him access to their world of imagination. He can only achieve that when he displays his human characteristics and does not go walking around like some unworldly fool. The 'contact clown' is an understanding clown and not a mocking clown.

The term 'contact-clown' applies to a clown who is able to make contact using:

+ Attention
+ Respect
+ Love
+ Compassion
+ Helpfulness

Clowning out of helpfulness is also one of the main principles of the so-called Clown Doctors. These are clowns who perform for very sick children in hospitals. Before these clowns enter a room, they are informed about the child's condition. When they are standing behind the window of the hospital room, they observe how the patient responds to their presence. Are they allowed to come in or should they better come back some other time? It is the sick child who is in charge, the child indicates what he needs, and the clowns deliver. Below you can read the recollection of Clown Doctor 'Blush':

"In room 3, a little girl is lying in bed. I look through the window in the door and I see two braids, a bit of pink pyjama and a teddy bear sitting on the edge of her bed. The bear looks a bit worn; I think it has been cuddled a lot. The girl takes a shy peek from beneath her blanket. She just got back from having surgery. Her mother is sitting beside her bed. For a moment there is contact, the girl has seen me. That is to say, the girl has seen Blush, because that is my name as a clown. Blush is a real sweetheart and sometimes she pretends to be a bit tough. She is naughty and playful, but more than anything else she is a vulnerable and uninhibited clown. Going inside straight away does not seem like a good idea. I had better build it up gently.
A spot on the window of the door desperately needs to be cleaned. With a small tissue I start to polish. It makes a squeaking sound. I glance at the girl again. Her face is completely visible now and she is watching what I am doing. I feel comfortable enough to go into the room to see whether I am able to clean the window from the other side. I am inside the room now and everything is okay. I continue rubbing the tissue against the window, but now I make small noises in doing so: blowing, splattering and squeaky noises. From the corner of my eye I see the girl sitting up. She curiously looks my direction, still a bit shy. Her mother smiles.
My movements become bigger and I start cleaning spots on the walls and the sink. I keep getting closer to the girl and suddenly I hear her say, 'here on my bed there is another spot!' Surprised I look up; we are in this together now. I wipe the frame of her bed. 'There is another one... and there', she points. I clean like a madwoman!

It is good to see that she feels in control. Would I be able to take another step closer in our contact? I cry out, 'hey, mummy has some dirt on her nose!' I wipe her mother's nose and the girl starts to laugh. Now I see a dirty spot on the girl's nose and I ask her if I can wipe it off… but now I asked too much. For a moment it is exciting, but then she answers, 'No, but I see a dirty spot on your nose!' 'Oh, no!' I yell, 'could you get it off?'

Now I am really close by and she gently wipes the spot off my red nose. A short, kind moment of contact and silence. It touches me. It feels special that I am allowed to come so close and that she is really completely distracted from her being ill. Now that all the spots have been cleaned, it is time to say goodbye. I walk through the doorway and wipe the last spot off the window. Then I turn my head once more to look and wave at her. The girl is sitting up in her bed with a big smile on her face and waves back.

Feeling satisfied, I walk into the long hallway. I was able to give her a lovely moment of distraction. And what a present that is to me!" (22)

This account shows how Blush starts by magnetic playing and more and more turns to electric playing. First she tries to gain the little girl's trust, and when that is established it is possible to make further contact.

Performing for demented seniors has almost the same approach. Although these people are often less active or capable of indicating what they need than sick children, the main principle for making contact remains the same. With them, a clown will also search for a childlike togetherness, something the nursing staff cannot do, for the lack of time or empathy, or perhaps also from a sense of shame. It is very important for a clown to delicately make use of the senses: giving a gentle touch, blowing a beautiful soap bubble, humming a well-known tune from the past, or spraying a pleasant scent. The responses are often surprising and heart-warming.

"It shows that approaching a demented person as a clown suits a demented person who has passed the first stage of dementia; he will surrender to the process of returning to the past. In the first stage of dementia, a person is too much stuck in inner conflict and wants to focus on reality as much as possible. However, in the later stages, most people have a need for primary and sensory experiences such as caressing, touching and holding. Accompanying them in their emotions and, in this way, making contact, is the fundamental idea of a clown. He searches, sometimes with a word, sometimes with an action, sometimes with an object, for a link to the imaginary world of the demented person at that particular moment. From that – often fragile – contact, the clown can try to make a link to the present. In working with this method, inner peace is created for the demented person and his or her self-esteem is restored. This contributes to reducing problematic behaviour and improves the quality of life." (23)

More and more, clowns can work wonders, as can be read in the report of clown Maretty on her first day of clowning for demented seniors in the ward of a nursing home:

"A man sits at a table in the living room, he is sleeping. I go and sit next to him, I tap him on the shoulder; he continues sleeping. I gently poke his leg with my finger, he looks sideways. Our eyes meet for a moment, then I look away and he closes his eyes again. This goes on three times, then he keeps watching and a smile appears on his face. He looks at me and shrugs questioningly. I draw a figure on the table with my finger. He smiles, surprised. 'I don't understand what you mean.' I repeat the movement, now he starts drawing too. While we draw, our fingers get tangled up and our other hands join in. We have continuous eye-contact and our hands twirl around each other. Then I pretend that I want to kiss his hand, but that I am afraid to. I keep getting closer and continue looking at him, and he looks back with a smile on his face. We play like this for a while. He strokes my cheek. Our laughter and our play grow together. Then I say goodbye,

I wave until I am out of sight, and I see the man strains his body to watch the last of me.

Later I make a conversation with a nurse who had been watching us. She had seen that, minutes after I had left, the man still had a blissful look on his face. She had asked him if he had liked it. His answer: 'Yes, she is sweet, she gave me a boost.' While writing it down, it touches me. So what am I doing over there? I give people boosts. What a great feeling." (24)


↔ *Honesty* ↔


*"Being a clown is not about learning tricks, it is about unlearning survival techniques. When we play and take down our masks, we will find our true selves. The original link between the adult and the inner child is restored." (1)*


Apparently we lie about 35 times (!) per day, lying meaning 'not telling the truth'. This often happens automatically or because we do not feel like telling the whole story. To 'How are you doing?', for instance, we almost always answer with 'Good!' even if this is not the case. For a clown it is different: he only cares about what he feels and experiences in the present moment, without any additional thoughts. And whether he is doing okay or not, he will tell you about it honestly and sometimes extensively.

I notice that I have become more comfortable in giving my opinion, and that I feel less afraid of having a different opinion than someone else, or having an argument. I can see now that this does not necessarily mean the end of a friendship. It actually gives me more insights into the value and essence of a relationship. I have become less of a spectator to my own life and I live and act more from my core, from my heart. I am also able to say 'no' more easily when I feel 'no', as a result of which I am more capable of indicating my boundaries. For example, sometimes when I used to lie on the sofa, exhausted, my little son Steef would ask me if I wanted to play a game. Despite the fact I did not really want to, I said 'yes'. To do him a favour. However, this way it was not fair for either of us. He saw that I did not really want to play and felt guilty about that. I was also not fair to myself because I did not choose what I desired, namely to rest.

*"Communication hurts. If it does not hurt, no communication has taken place. You should not make promises. There is no point. Everybody does that. You need to tell people the truth. And truth is nothing but pain." (25)*

Some years ago, I decided for myself that from then on I wanted to live as honestly as I could. Through several experiences I came to see that I no longer wanted to hide myself behind good manners, half truths or plain lies, but that I wanted to live from my heart. This is not always appreciated because honesty can be hard to bear. I get support from something Titus Brandsma (a Dutch priest who was murdered in World War II) once said: 'Whoever wants to win the world over for higher ideals must have the courage to enter into conflict with her.' For me, honesty is such a higher ideal.

I once saw an important Roland Garros tennis match on television. Russian player Marat Safin corrected the umpire at a crucial moment by saying that his opponent's serve was not out, but in. Partially thanks to this he lost the game and with that the whole match. The commentator was stunned, but also full of praise about the integrity of this professional. Personally, I still suffer from the fact that, long ago, I had not been honest about a wrong call from the umpire thanks to which I won an important tennis match. Where I had always been honest before, this time I could not fight the temptation of the splendour that was awaiting me. Now I can't even remember where I put the trophy, but the bad memory remains.

## ⇥ The ego ⇤

*"While people have a natural tendency to withdraw themselves when they have experienced a painful situation, a clowning course asks them to do exactly the opposite. The movement outward is a vulnerable step, in which the struggle between the ego and the higher self becomes visible. Clowning instructor Roelant de Vletter explains that 'the ego is always busy with its fears: the fear to fail, not to be seen, to be rejected; or it is busy with the urge to do something as well as possible. When you are in touch with your higher self, and perform from there, it actually does not matter what others think. Feelings are there to be felt and to be expressed. That is enough for the higher self. It comes down to the suggestion that during a performance, the ego should constantly yield to what is'."* (26)

Your ego resides in your head and prevents you from showing your real self. When you are born, the ego has not yet developed; you can only feel. Gradually, you will need your ego for survival, but as you grow older it is valuable to try to let go of your ego bit by bit and start living from your feelings more. That also means to stop being attached to status, giving free rein to your assertiveness, or competing with others. Loss or profit, applause or failure, happiness or sadness... it is good to accept that things are the way they are. Only then can there be compassion for others and an opening for real connections. This is true for you as a person and therefore also for you as a clown. It clears the way towards showing your authenticity.

The clown is not the type to want to win games at any cost. Since he is not burdened with an ego that forces him to want to be in charge, he does not act out of self-interest; instead he follows his guts. To many people, achievement and status are very important and losing is a painful affair. This is caused by fear. Fear of not being approved of if you do not achieve things. Winning and the need to always be right is related to confirmation of the ego. A strong ego can help you reach your goals, perform with excellence, and show character. That is wonderful, but the question remains whether that alone is fulfilling? Can something else exist next to it? Something vulnerable, sensitive, and compassionate?

*"To be able to show compassion one must let go of the ego; one must take oneself out of the centre of his or her world and place someone else there instead. Not many people are capable of doing this. People want to be right and show no compassion; the ego is stronger." (27)*

Like an uninhibited child, a clown embraces life fully, open and accepting, in a way that we adults can only be jealous of. Having a competitive spirit or seeking approval are out of the question.

When there is no ego, there is only love.

In the past, after I finished a performance, course, or workshop, I often fished for approval, especially when I thought everything had gone very well. Insecurity caused me to search for confirmation to feed my ego: 'You see, Ton, you are an excellent teacher.' Nowadays I don't do that any more (or at least not consciously). I do not want to be dependent on other people's opinions. Everybody is different and has unique opinions on all sorts of things, so you can never please everybody. I believe that the most important thing is that inside myself, I feel satisfied.

Challenges that help you let go of your ego more:

+ Helping someone without expecting a thank-you.
+ Giving money to charity without telling this to others.
+ Giving a performance, free of charge, for charity (for instance as a clown).
+ Doing volunteer work.
+ Not striving for being the best.

+ Nobly admitting it when you cannot do something or made a mistake.
+ Not reacting negatively if someone does you wrong (bearing).
+ Granting other people applause that was actually meant for you.

## ↦ Living from the heart ↤

Living exclusively for yourself is not fulfilling. A human being's existence is enhanced through contact with his fellow men. Joy and others' grief also have an effect on you. By living your life with an open heart, special encounters can take place. Open communication is only possible when there is a mutual respect for each other's boundaries. There are clowns that follow you in the streets and imitate your way of moving around. The moment you look behind you, they walk away. Of course they magnify your movements and exaggerate the image of you. But they are not honest, they make fun at your expense. To me it is of vital importance that both parties feel comfortable around each other and that they can enjoy themselves because of that trust. It takes two to tango.

*"A clown accepts himself, others, and the world, exactly the way they are. He is just himself, not occupied with obligations, achieving things, or surpassing himself. Nor does he judge what is right or what is wrong. He reacts to that which comes his way with honesty and from his heart." (1)*

A clown wants to meet everyone; he does not differentiate between appearances, gender or race. This life attitude of wanting to connect to a person just the way he or she is, is called an 'attached' attitude. The opposite attitude is 'detached'. It is not that difficult to connect with only beautiful or easy people, but can you do the same with ugly or unpleasant people? You can intensely enjoy a gorgeous rose, but what about thorny weeds? Do you give up because you think it is unsightly? Ugliness is just a perception, often supported by a majority, but that does not automatically mean it is universal. What does it feel like for *you*? What do *you* like? For example, at home, you could try looking at something you think is dirty or hideous, for instance that worn-out curtain, that slanted side table, or that well-thumbed book. When you look beyond the surface and try to see the beauty in it, you are more connected to reality. Reality the way you experience it without judgement.

The things I find hardest in life teach me the most. And exactly the people I am 'allergic' to, point out my own shortcomings. I get a clearer image of myself by seeking these people out instead of trying to avoid them. The mirror image they show me is not always a pretty one. But facing my own weaknesses brings forward some great insights.

An attitude of judging too fast has its origins in the past. What kind of pain has remained as a result of a lack of freedom (conditional love) and denial of your own personality? Old convictions and judgements are embedded in all our actions and repeatedly surface in places. This results in a constant search for confirmation from the group you are a part of. Getting this feels safe and pleasant, but it actually means that you have let yourself down. You are not living from your heart but out of fear.

I remember one day I was walking in a park with a group of course participants, when suddenly a car came our way, driving on the footpath. I nonverbally made clear, by shaking my head and raising my arms, that it was an outrage that people could not even walk in the park peacefully nowadays. The car stopped and the driver asked me what my problem was. He explained that he had just delivered some gear for a performance that was to take place at the pond that afternoon. I felt deeply ashamed of myself inside. I had already judged him without even asking the why-question. Ouch! These are the kinds of incidents I find painful, but they also help me to get more understanding for other people.

As a clown, you directly and openly show what is going on inside of you. By feeling your emotions deeply, a lot gets put to motion, and old scars may come to the surface. It gives relief when emotions can find their way out, and by sharing them with others, the pain can be lifted and makes room for you, your glorious child, and your kind clown. Does this make clowning a form of therapy? I don't think so. There is no need to tell anybody anything about the background of your emotions, nor about your childhood experiences. You only look at the emotions that are present in this moment. Without any doubt, the outcome clowning can have therapeutic effects, but this is not the same thing.

*"A doctor makes his bitter pills tasty by sweetening them. A clown makes life's bitterness palatable by making jokes. A human being can open up through the use of humour, even for the deepest pains. So that together with the joy, the grief, too, is released and expressed."* (1)

↦ *Conclusion* ↤

The fear of showing your true self keeps you from standing in the spotlight. It is the fear of showing your vulnerable side, the fear of being truly seen, and the fear of being judged by your shortcomings. Fear gets your defence mechanisms going, such as gossiping about the neighbours, criticising foreigners, voting out candidates from television shows, and so on. These things keep us out of harm's way and we save our egos, but this way we do forfeit love. A clown *is* love; he lives and performs from his heart. He is always thinking in terms of resemblances instead of differences. By first saying 'yes' to himself, he can subsequently say 'yes' to others, just the way they are. This opens the door to universal love. The love that is returned to me during my performances touches me more than words can tell. Therefore,

I see it as my great personal challenge to go through life more like my clown would: open-minded and without fear.

*"In order to be a good clown, we must let go of our defence mechanisms and show ourselves with all our peculiarities and our vulnerability." (1)*

Vulnerability is inextricably linked to love and makes sure that we dare to show our flaws and shortcomings as well as our qualities. We can do this out of compassion for ourselves and through acceptance that we are just the way we are. Living with an open heart makes you gentle and opens the hearts of others, which is something children do without being aware of it. Selfless love gives rise to a deeper connection to the people around us. Clowns give us a great gift by showing us how we can achieve this. They help us get past our shame and live in freedom, and they teach us how to play like cheerful children. How we can make contact with the people around us from heart to heart. They invite us to act without being afraid of making mistakes, and show us that there is nothing wrong with following our impulses.

When clowning, you are automatically confronted with your own boundaries, because it is difficult to show your vulnerability, clumsiness or shyness in public. But it is also beneficial to experience and accept obstacles: you are fine the way you are. If you manage to do this, you can push back those boundaries step by step. And communicate even more openly and honestly. Performing from your heart. When we dare to listen to our desires, we consequentially give space to our inner child: a child who needs to play and discover. A child who lives life with love, naturally.

*"I will try to radiate some of the love, the true love for people, that I have inside of me, wherever I go. I do not want to be special, I just want to try to be that person who, deep down inside of me, is still looking for full development." (28)*

Every heartbeat lets you know that you are alive. All the thoughts and fantasies about the past or the future keep you away from the joy of unique moment. We can try to put the pain and frustrations of our hurt child behind us. We cannot change the past, but we can change the way we are living right now.

I wholeheartedly hope that his book will help you forward in performing as a clown. A human clown. Hopefully, your desire to openly show yourself will triumph, and your fear of showing yourself will disappear. Experience the excitement of walking around wearing funny clothes, wearing your red nose, without too many attributes. You will have to cope with what you have, which is yourself, including all your belongings and your peculiarities. That might be more than you think. If you simply make clear that you would like to get to know people, they will open up to you. From my own experience: a clown has but to raise his hand, and a salutation comes back at him almost every time.

# ↔ *10 clownish ways of living* ↔

Be terribly curious

Live in the here and now

Feel and share

Communicate openly

Reduce your ego

Cherish your inner child

Let go of control

Say a heartfelt 'yes!'

Develop your limitless creativity

Always be your true self

# 7. Impressions of course participants

*m*eeting my clown touched me in a way that is not easily expressed in words. The words honesty, playfulness, and boundaries keep coming back to me. During my clowning courses I saw that a lot of emotions were released, such as amazement, sadness, tension, happiness and frustration. After the courses I would receive post, emails, and telephone calls. I decided to find a way to use this and I invited participants to write down their impressions and emotions.

These contributions give a good picture of the diversity of experiences. It shows what clowning can do for you. They are personal outpourings, which show a glimpse of the inner child of each and every one of them.

I don't have pictures of my clown and I can't conjure her on command, but she's always there, behind a curtain. I can't just open the curtain like peek-a-boo. She will only come of her own accord, when she feels it's safe.... Or when an emotion is too big to keep inside... I don't know how else to describe it. But it feels good that I get space to show her, and maybe that's enough; to know that it is possible.... And then it doesn't really have to anymore.... Do you understand? She wants to be allowed to be there, but if she knows that she can, she doesn't need so much attention anymore.... I made a start to write you that she exists. And it is incredible that you welcome her so much. That touches me. Perhaps I can quickly say something in the group circle, and see if she will want to show herself some evening... the less I am occupied with her, the sooner she comes, I've noticed.

Now I am much closer to myself, but every time I am untrue to myself, I feel much pain. How is that possible, I thought? Apparently you don't experience a gaping hole as a painful wound, but a tiny scratch can be quite uncomfortable. That's the way it works.... The closer I get to where I want to be, the more conscious I am of the distance. It itches, that's how you should see it, I believe. I have an itching wound and I am not allowed to scratch at the scabs...and I am so impatient... grumble.... But the itch in itself is a good sign. Clowning puts lots in motion and makes me aware of the road ahead of me.

*Betty*

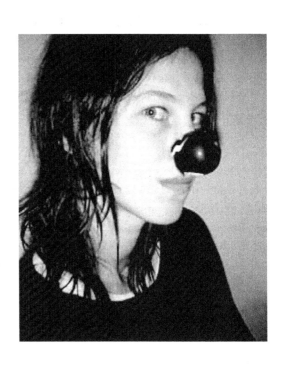

The strength of a clown is that he is so simple.
This makes a clown pure and real.
No difficult words, no posh clothes, no socially adjusted behaviour.
A clown does what he feels like,
and the fun part is that others will enjoy along.

The heavy things in life; these a clown does not know yet.
Even sadness and anger are very simple for a clown.
Is a clown sad, he will cry.
Is a clown angry, he will cry out.
He will not hide anything for his companions, who feel compelled
to emphasise with him.
The other way around, a clown will emphasise with others, naturally.

In order to live like a clown, I do not need a red nose.
Sometimes I wear it anyway,
so people around me understand me better.

*Debora*

This week at my training we worked with the theme 'your inner clown' for the first time. I thought, 'great, we'll have some laughs...' But no, my first experience with clowning was exactly the other side of the medal.... I had to cry loads and felt a need to flee; I was confronted with my fear to let my deepest feelings out, and at the same time with the necessity to approach my inner child with gentleness, and not to judge.... Phew, quite a lot to process, but it keeps me busy and it inspires me to express myself artistically.

It is a relief to be allowed to be human, with all that I am. That I may cry if I feel like it, or laugh, really hard, if that's what I want. If people want to walk around with a mask, let them, if that's what makes them feel good. This gives me strength! I never dared to be myself before; I never learnt this at home when I was younger, and there was (or is) always that sense of shame. I am currently in an uncomfortable conflict with a colleague, who pours a whole load of rubbish over me, about what she believes I am. And she feels like she can't say anything to me, because I'll cry.... She thinks that's stupid and immature.... But retrospectively, this conflict, however painful, teaches me a lot: nobody can take myself away from me, and she will have to make do with who I am. I am not going to adapt to her wishes, and I am not going to hide myself behind a mask of false friendliness, if that's not what I feel inside.

I would have never thought that the subject 'clown' would have looked like this, and that it would apply so well to me as a human being. I always thought that a clown only belonged in a circus, where only children go to.... Or clown doctors, who cheer up hospitalised children. But that a clown is so close by.... is a surprise! Something completely new; a new challenge, an addition to my inner child, which touched me so deeply and still does!

*Ineke*

I am getting more and more convinced that there is a clown hidden away inside of me, deep down. Apparently now is the time for it to come out, bit by bit. At last I am allowed to be a child....

Two years ago, to counter the effects of my work (a lot of thinking work), I wanted to get closer to my feelings. I was at odds with myself and with others. Subsequently I went to do a course with you, Ton. I found the first course to be very exciting! And also very pleasant. Some exercises came close to my inner core. They touched some tender chords; chords from my childhood, which I was trying to deal with. They loosened up a lot. For that second clowning course I did need a bit of a push, but I followed it with lots of fun and inner confidence. There were tears of joy as I went home afterwards. I was especially glad that I could just let myself go and let the child in me emerge.

Yes, it was as easy as that.... Me, the quiet child, shy, and insecure, always worrying whether others are okay, always at the back at musicals in primary school, never daring to stand in front of a group. And now I enjoy clowning! The past two years I got more and more of a taste for being a child again. I attended more courses and actually really started performing as a clown! I find having small encounters fantastic, whether in the streets, at parties, or at special occasions. My performance at the Moscow State Circus was a beautiful experience. I was happy as a child! Clowning encouraged me to take on new challenges, for instance at work. Saying 'yes', going for it, and being open to new things. It costs a lot of energy but it did work out more and more, which boosted my confidence. And I worry less about people in my immediate sur-roundings. I also met a lot of wonderful people through clowning. I consider that to be very special, all those different backgrounds and childlike qualities. It always feels like a warm bath when we meet.

When I reflect upon the past time period, I see that my clown is liberating my inner child. It was hidden far away, but now I may be a child at last.

*Nel*

I follow my own path, because I follow my feelings and my heart. It is a path that doesn't coincide with the one that is promoted and smoothed out by our society, so it is sometimes winding and lonely.

As a child I already felt, 'Why did I end up here? Do I have to live here, in this horror?' I found the world and our society complete nonsense; they clashed with my feelings. I did realise I had to be here, and make the most of it…just by being who I am and doing whatever feels good for me.

I see myself as somebody who is still really very much child, or better: somebody who is simply herself. It seems to me the simplest way to be. I wouldn't know how to be different! For many people this is apparently very difficult. They have lost themselves somewhere along the way, and I don't understand how they can still live that way, and not miss themselves terribly!

*Annick Thijs*

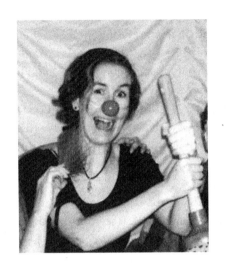

What is clowning? You will not learn how best to paint your face, you will not learn how to juggle, you will not learn how to model balloons. No cracking jokes, no whoopee cushions. You will learn to be present with your full attention, present with yourself and others. You learn to see what you would otherwise not see as an adult. It is a process that makes me a bit reluctant to share how it was and what we did and oh how much fun it was, because then this will just become an enormous you-had-to-be-there story.

It does have everything to do with letting go. I do want to share that. Because, man, how adults get stuck in all sorts of things. Am I blushing? Do I look silly? I hope I am not drooling. Was my laughter too loud? Let it go! Because if you let it go you can let yourself go, and if you let go, a world of joy will open up to you; joy and compassion for yourself and others. A small paradise. Many people don't believe this exists, or that it does, but only in the afterlife. And there we go, what grownup thoughts again. While you can be in the here and now. When you realise how it works, and that you can be in the now, and enjoy the world openly and with a big fat wink, it is here.

*Gwen*

I found it was difficult to let out whatever would surface, because I had the feeling that if people hire you as a clown, they would have expectations. Now I have seen that these expectations are created by myself, and if you play your cards openly, you will truly see what kind of expectations are in the game, if any. During a wedding I set out without any props, which brought my clown's play back to the basics, and I was so stimulated by my surroundings that the entire performance reached high levels.

*Bram*

I really enjoyed the uninhibited and no-pressure acting. More than ten years ago, I studied theatre productions at a drama school. There we used to act as well (especially in the first two years), but I realise now that I had never actually been able to act like this without fear and shame. There was always pressure: can I do this? Will they think I am good enough? Do they like me? In fact, it was quite frustrating and there was always this insecurity…I would always compare myself to others, and feel a kind of jealousy when others did get appraisal and were called 'stunning'. Of course there was a reason why I chose to be a director. I used to always say that I wasn't a real actor…but what is a real actor?

One Saturday night I woke up in the middle of the night and I couldn't get back to sleep. Suddenly there was an awareness deep down inside of me that I only needed to be myself, nothing more. Being who I am and showing this and reacting honestly to what I notice inside of me; that is being a real clown. A real clown can make very clear what improvisation and performing are about. Acting is playing, truly playing. Acting on a stage is pretending to act, and that is very different from 'being' a clown, or, better yet, accepting the clown inside yourself.
A clown always says 'yes'; he accepts what is happening. At the drama school, I had always been taught these things in a very technical manner, like it was something outside of me. I learned to suppress my own feelings in a professional way, so they couldn't interfere with the character I was playing and I would be able to transform. I acted beyond myself, not from the heart. I considered my fears, insecurities and frustration to be unprofessional and I didn't allow myself to feel them.
I actually spent a part of my life trying to hide and make myself invisible. It wasn't until the last few years that I started searching for a way of connecting more to other people and the world around me, to show myself. I have let go of a lot of fear…

During the clowning weekend, it was an epiphany to realise that I could actually be myself (including all my experiences and feelings) and that because of this I could perform with so much pleasure...and that it even led to a satisfying performance! Funny how a mask (which is what I experience the nose to be) liberated me to take off my own masks and reveal myself.

It is hard to express how happy I feel because of all of this, and how curious I am to get to know my inner clown, of whom I already caught a glimpse and whom I hope to get to know better in the future. While performing, I experienced a connection between myself and the group, which created a beautiful interaction. Something else happened that rose above me; it came from a sense of openness, an existence, a presence in the moment. It was a kind of flow, life-energy, whatever you want to call it, and it touched me very deeply.

*Lieke*

# Bibliography

1. In this book, I use quotes about clowning, which I have gathered throughout the years. In most cases, I do not know whom they belong to. Should someone recognise a quote and have a problem with me using them, you can send an e-mail to ton@clownerie.nl

2. Part of a note about clowning from Jos Gebbinck, senior trainer at the SBI, an organisation for training and advice.

3. *The world of clowns* / George Bishop

4. *De therapeut als clown* / Ernst Knijff (own translation)

5. *Celebrate life!* / Leo Buscaglia (paraphrased)

6. *The Mastery of Love* / Don Miguel Ruiz (paraphrased)

7. *The drama of the gifted child* / Alice Miller (paraphrased)

8. *Blij dat ik twijfel* / Hans Oosterom (own translation)

9. *Levenskunst* / compiled by Winkler Prins editorship (own translation)

10. *Homecoming* / John Bradshaw (paraphrased)

11. *Wie zijn ik?* / Goos Geursen — The first sentence has been quoted by the author from *The magic of conflict* by Thomas Crum. (own translation)

12. *Manifesting - Create your own reality* / Ninsandeh Neta (paraphrased)

13. *Manifesting - Create your own reality* / Ninsandeh Neta (paraphrased)

14. *Essays in love* / Alain de Botton

15. Interview with Katja Schuurman, Volkskrant 24 December 2005 (own translation)

16. *Het lichaam liegt nooit* / Ted Troost (own translation)

17. *The fear of freedom* / Erich Fromm (paraphrased)

18. *The Art of Happiness* / Howard Cutler & the Dalai Lama. The quote itself comes from Shakyamuni.

19. *Living, loving, learning* / Leo Buscaglia

20. *In Lucia's Eyes* / Arthur Japin

21. *Wie zijn ik?* / Goos Geursen (own translation)

22. Account by Wendy Riemslag, January 2009 (own translation)

23. Frans van Lith (own translation)

24. Account by Maretty van den Mosselaar, September 2004 (own translation)
25. *The Jewish Messiah* /Arnon Grunberg (paraphrased)
26. Interview with Roelant de Vletter in the magazine Jonas, September 2005 (own translation)
27. Interview with Karen Armstrong in Academy Magazine, spring 2006 (own translation)
28. *Etty — the letters and diaries of Etty Hillesum 1941-1943* (paraphrased)

# Exercises

## Photographs:

OÖ Berufsfotografen, Linz, *page 34*
Thomas Haberstroh, Vienna, *page 40*
Onno van Geuns, *page 101, 142*
Huub Beckers, *page 128*

## Illustrations:

Ida Lorbach, *pages 14, 51, 60, 85, 166*
Lidwien Buné, *pages 132, 133*

Ida Lorbach has made coloured postcards from her illustrations. You can look at these beautiful paintings and order them via *www.idalorbach.de*

CPSIA information can be obtained
at www.ICGtesting.com
Printed in the USA
FSOW04n1049040117
29203FS